THE BIG QUESTIONS
God

Mark Vernon is a journalist, broadcaster and author of several books. He is the editor-in-chief of the *Chambers Dictionary of Beliefs and Religions*, an honorary research fellow at Birkbeck, University of London, and has degrees in physics and theology and a PhD in philosophy. He used to be a priest in the Church of England, left a convinced atheist, though then had to admit he is too drawn by the big spiritual questions not to take religious traditions and practice seriously – a journey he has written about in his book *How to be an Agnostic*.
He is a keen blogger at www.markvernon.com.

The Big Questions confronts the fundamental problems of science and philosophy that have perplexed enquiring minds throughout history, and provides and explains the answers of our greatest thinkers. This ambitious series is a unique, accessible and concise distillation of humanity's best ideas.

Series editor **Simon Blackburn** is Professor of Philosophy at the University of Cambridge, Research Professor of Philosophy at the University of North Carolina and one of the most distinguished philosophers of our day.

Titles in *The Big Questions* series include:

PHILOSOPHY
PHYSICS
THE UNIVERSE
MATHEMATICS
GOD
EVOLUTION

THE BIG QUESTIONS

God

Mark Vernon

SERIES EDITOR
Simon Blackburn

Quercus

Contents

INTRODUCTION

One day a philosopher was asked to define religion. Immediately he begged for time to prepare an answer. The time lapsed, and he returned asking for more. That period passed and he requested another postponement. And then another. And another. At last those asking understood the delays. The philosopher regarded the task as well-nigh impossible, but he still wanted time to contemplate the question. It was too rich to put aside.

This parable, told by the philosopher Søren Kierkegaard, neatly captures why the searching reflected in the answers to the big questions of this book is so fascinating. To ask about God and faith, science and the soul, the spiritual and suffering is to ask about the issues that matter most to humans. It is to participate in the quest that has inspired the world's most beautiful buildings, the world's most stirring music, humanity's most profound intuitions and thought. It is to ask about what makes us human. 'Religion to me has always been the wound, not the bandage', reflected the playwright Dennis Potter, which is to say that the religious person is one who wishes to face the imponderable and tender aspects of life.

Philosophy and reason play a vital part. They are the essential tools of discernment, the careful processes by which experiences, insights and traditions can be assimilated and assessed, and the next step forward charted. They help us pay attention to what goes on in our inner lives and in the world around us. As the great physicist Werner Heisenberg noted, we are lucky to live in a time when our perception of the cosmos is in rapid flux. He advised us to stay open-minded, spiritually as well as empirically, and to check our own view of life, deepened by study and meditation, against the careful results of the great search called science. The mechanical atoms of yesterday's physics have morphed into the lively quantum fields of today's. The blind struggle known as Darwinian evolution is being reinterpreted as a cosmic striving for complexity, emergence and the most extraordinary fact of all: that there is something, not nothing, and that in us, that something can gaze back at the universe that nurtured it.

This, I suspect, is why God has not died, why the spiritual life still draws us. Religious traditions face major challenges, so much so that even those who go to churches, temples, synagogues or mosques may prefer to call themselves 'spiritual but not religious'. But ours is an age of the soul too, in the sense that ecological crises are awakening a desire for a better relationship with nature, or in the sense that the well-being delivered by the copious material goods we can purchase also prompts the thought that there must be more to life, followed by the question: where might that more be found? Faith is often taxing, and is ridiculed by some. But then, as Albert Einstein noted, 'God is subtle but he is not malicious.'

This book is designed to show that some of the oldest questions concerned with spirituality, religion and God can be asked afresh in our day to reveal new and striking possibilities. What we might discover for ourselves also resonates powerfully with the insights of the best theologians and wisest souls of the past. It is as if something fundamental is being excavated; like having a familiar work of art explained, so that it suddenly looks as if you are seeing it properly for the first time. It is as if we live in a moment when the quest for God or spirit is unfolding for us anew.

Perhaps every generation feels a bit like this. 'What do I love when I love my God?' asked St Augustine. 'Tend within to the opening of your heart', advised Rumi. Or you may feel more like William James, the psychologist of religion, who declared that his study of the variety of religious experiences found amongst human beings was his 'religious act'. So I hope your questioning and contemplation are nurtured here.

CAN REASON PROVE THE EXISTENCE OF GOD?

Why 'proofs' almost don't fail, and how that is helpful

There is no rational basis for belief in God, it is often insisted. Reason knows that night follows day. Logic fails to underpin faith. But is that right? A closer look at the so-called 'proofs' for God reveals something perhaps unexpected. To see what that is, first take a step back.

Living Christianity

Christianity offers philosophers not one but two patron saints. Whether or not they seek or desire the intercession of these holy individuals is debatable. However, there is wit and insight in the patronage of both.

The first is Justin Martyr. Born in the sleepy backwater of Samaria in the second century AD, he spoke Greek, and so made his way to Roman civilization, where he sat at the feet of the philosophers. He first tried out the Stoics, the most successful of the schools of the time, though they did not satisfy him. They were the closest the ancient world came to champions of self-help, and that inclined them to be obsessed with themselves, with little of interest to say about God. So Justin turned to an Aristotelian teacher, though that did not last beyond the old curmudgeon's obsession with fixing the right fee.

Next he reached out to the Pythagoreans, who had a fascination with the mysteries of mathematics and music. That was appealing in theory, only Justin found that geometry and playing the lyre were beyond him. So he left them too.

Eventually he ended up with the Platonists. They offered a lot. In particular, he was drawn to their ideas about divinity. They had a notion that there is a high God, and that although this aspect remains beyond the reach of human comprehension, the divine energy – or Logos – overflows to touch the souls of men and women. It was an immensely rich theology. Justin loved it and he stuck with it, until one day he was walking along the seashore at Ephesus and he met a wise man. The two started talking, and before the day was out, he had moved on again. He had been converted to Christianity. The divine energy of the Platonists, this Logos, had become flesh, the sage told him. You could encounter it in the person of Jesus.

Justin remained loyal to what he had learnt before. He wore the philosopher's cloak for the rest of his life. But by now he really thought that truth-seekers needed to step out of the confines of pure reasoning and embrace a first-hand knowledge of reality. He might have agreed with William James, who noted that philosophy works out the cost of the meal called life and can

> *Philosophy works out the cost of the meal called life and can write you a bill, but religion offers you the meal itself.*

write you a bill, but religion offers you the meal itself. Christianity, Justin concluded, offered the richest fare he had tasted so far. (He also argued that the ancient schools of philosophy were always wrangling amongst themselves, which hardly commends them – though in so saying, he conveniently forgot that the new schools of Christianity had form too when it came to bickering and squabbling.)

The second patron saint is Catherine of Alexandria, after whom Catherine wheels are named. She was born into a noble family and achieved great learning, so much so that she informed her parents she would only marry a man who outshone her own beautiful intelligence. No such husband could be found, until Catherine discovered Christianity. She found her perfect match in Jesus Christ.

As if that were not demonstration enough of Christianity's superiority, she then proceeded to convert dozens of philosophers the emperor sent to test her, catching a further soul for Christ in the figure of the empress herself. Her victory was rewarded by the philosophers being martyred before Catherine was tied to a wheel and tortured before being beheaded.

> *The living wisdom of Christianity is greater than that of any dry philosophy because it is focused in the life of a person, Jesus Christ.*

Catherine's legend could be, in part, apocryphal. The earliest record of her life only reaches back to the ninth century. Justin Martyr, though, is an important historical and theological figure. But either way, you get the point. The living wisdom of Christianity is greater than that of any dry philosophy because it is focused in the life of a person, Jesus Christ.

Faith and reason

That is a deliberately provocative and perceptive insight to remember in any debate about the proofs for the existence of God. Religious faiths are inevitably systematized, refined and tried by the deployment of reason. But their origin and source is not rational – which is not to say that it is irrational either. Rather, faith is born of an awareness. Its wellspring is not logic but life.

The Buddha saw into the suffering nature of existence and constructed a way of life to surpass it. Moses realized that God was not in the idols and pillars, the earthquakes and winds as the pagans believed; God is to be found in the darkness of the cloud, the silence of heaven. Muhammad was powerfully persuaded that to know Allah, the warring tribalism of the Arabian desert should yield to a life marked by mercy. Jesus became keenly aware that in the kingdom of God, the first would be last, servants would be exalted, and the rule of love meant you must be ready to die for it. Other religions, like Hinduism, have no fixed set of doctrines, but draw on the experience, forgotten in prehistory, of dozens of ancient cultures.

And God Blessed the Seventh Day and Sanctified It by William Blake. Blake is just one religious artist who tries to show God without losing a sense of divine mystery.

This is to say that, so far as believers are concerned, reason serves the revelation that animates the heart of faith. Reason cannot become the master of faith, and if it tries to, it becomes tyrannical, sucking the life out of it with its cool calculations. Conversely, faith is not the slave of reason. Faith is the product of educated spiritual passion.

Keeping reason in its place has served religious traditions well, though not, as the sceptic might suspect, by ensuring that faith is impervious to philosophical probing and by throwing smokescreens around the credulous. Religious traditions do, in fact, evolve as they engage with the philosophies that surround them. There are countless examples. Within a few years of Jesus's

11

death, Paul had changed the practice of the faith that Jesus had lived because it became impractical, in the Roman world, to insist on the Jewish dietary laws that Jesus had obeyed. No small part of Paul's surviving letters is devoted to making his case. Alternatively, theologians routinely explore and exploit philosophical ideas in their attempts to deepen their understanding of their faith. Justin Martyr, for example, used the Platonic and Stoic idea of the Logos to deepen his sense of the divine person he believed he met in the Christ. It is a principle immortalized by the motto of Anselm: 'Faith seeking understanding'.

Today, in debates about belief, protagonists may admit to being disturbed by faith. They suspect that it is deliberately, obstinately irrational. Part of the confusion stems from misunderstandings about the nature of faith. Sceptics may take it to mean belief on the basis of authority or third-party witness, rather than evidence; or, more antagonistically, belief in spite of the evidence: blind faith. But as Anselm insists, merely believing what you feel you ought to believe is deadening. True faith is a personal kind of commitment, based on the full range of experiences of which humans are capable. And we have many tools at our disposal for discerning what is true. The heart has its reasons. Beauty draws us with its allure. Stories, whilst often illogical and fictional, speak truly. Holy and admirable individuals stir us with a vision of a fuller human. There are tests of truth beyond logical consistency or indisputable certainty. By its fruits you know it, not by its roots, to recall another thought of William James.

> *True faith is a personal kind of commitment, based on the full range of experiences of which humans are capable.*

Using reason alone to find a way to the divine would be a bit like using guidebooks to discover a new country without ever rising from your seat. The discourses of reason are never going to produce momentous myths like the burning bush, the night journey to Jerusalem or the empty tomb. These are meaningful stories, not arguments, and they, rather than philosophical algebra, are the basic stuff of spiritual search and practice.

Aquinas's five ways

This perhaps explains one thing that is often overlooked in contemporary scuffles that try to prove or disprove the existence of God: namely that the great foundational documents of theist religions – the Bible, the Qur'an – don't contain any sustained attempts at proofs themselves. About the most enthusiasm they can muster for such debates is occasionally to pass comment, as when Psalm 14 observes, 'The fool has said in his heart that there is no God.'

However, the 'proofs' are with us, for good or ill, and are frequently referred to. So what can they tell us?

They include the ontological argument, associated with Anselm, alongside the 'five ways' of Thomas Aquinas – though the fact that Aquinas calls them 'ways' (*viae* in the Latin) immediately alerts us that he, like Anselm, is invoking a process of discovery that deploys but is not constrained by the narrower rigours of logic. It is pretty clear that Aquinas was, in fact, convinced that something called 'God' exists, if existence is the right way to put it. The tussle that his 'proofs' pursue, then, is more about what can and cannot be said about this ultimate Who or What. God was clearly present to him, and also almost entirely perplexing to him.

The first two of Aquinas's five ways argue that anything that moves needs a first mover to set it on its way, and similarly, anything that is caused needs a first cause. The 'unmoved mover' and the 'uncaused cause' are what we call God, Aquinas concludes – though the rigorous sceptic can immediately reply: why not have an infinite series of moving things, or an infinite chain of causes? Then you don't need an unmoved mover or an uncaused cause. Further, modern physics tells us that things that move don't need a prime mover: since Newton, it's been known that things keep moving in a uniform direction unless acted upon by an external force.

But Aquinas could come back in this way: ask yourself what an 'unmoved mover' might be, or an 'uncaused cause'. The phrases seem like contradictions, implying that any entity or force that could be described by them would tell you one thing about that entity or force above anything else. It would be beyond comprehension. Might that not be true of any being worthy of the name of God?

The third way is an argument about contingency and necessity, and might be boiled down to the issue of how you get something from nothing. This is a good question, a truly big one. After all, contingent things – such as we are, along with everything else in nature – will one day not be, and we might never have been either. And yet we, and everything else before and after us, do exist, at least for a while. So the logic of this proof runs like this: contingent existence itself must depend or rest upon something that is not contingent, which is to say, something that is necessary, else what is contingent will fall out of existence. For something cannot come out of nothing. So as there plainly is something, which we call the cosmos, there must also be something necessary, which could not not have been. This is what people speak of as God, Aquinas suggests. 'Proof' three. Except that non-theist religions like Buddhism insist that absolutely everything is conditioned and contingent, rising and falling like an everlasting wave. So it seems perfectly possible to imagine a cosmos full of contingent stuff and beings, existing entirely independently of any necessary being.

Another apparent failure – except that once again, the way does tell us one thing, and it turns out to be fundamental not just to this kind of theology but to a certain kind of science too. Consider something else that might be necessary: the set of natural laws, those principles that govern the universe. If you were to ask why they are as they are, as science does, then many people would conclude that they are as they are because there are no alternatives. Because the universe is as it is, they must be as they are. As Keith Ward points out in *The God Conclusion*, such necessary laws are precisely the kind of laws that cosmologists hope to find when they seek a so-called 'theory of everything'. This final theory would be a self-generating description that has to produce the universe in the way that it is, capable of bringing atoms, stars and intelligent life into being. Only then could it be an ultimate explanation because it is a necessary explanation.

But this raises a further issue. Ultimate, necessary explanations and laws could not exist on their own. Like sound waves, laws exist in a medium, and with laws the medium is called mind. When it comes to ultimate laws, therefore, you would need an ultimate mind to hold them. 'God is the cosmic mind whose content is the complete set of all mathematical truths', Ward continues. 'And once you have a cosmic mind, Aquinas clearly sees, you have a consciousness that can be aware of, evaluate, and discriminate between all the possibilities, mathematical and otherwise, that there are.'

It is a contentious line of thought, if highly abstract, and not of itself enough to elicit theistic belief: only the most autistic of rational minds would think natural laws or ultimate explanations worthy of worship. But it does show that the third 'proof', with its interest in necessity, opens up big and suggestive questions.

The fourth way concerns the nature of perfection, and states, in a simplified form, that the concept of perfection itself requires the existence of a being that actually embodies perfection, else how could imperfect humans have come up with the notion to start with? Without it, we would not even notice that everything was flawed, because life as we know it is blemished all the way down.

That doesn't follow, the sceptic says, because apart from anything else, who can describe what perfection is? No one. So a perfect God wouldn't help us with our understanding of perfection anyway.

Then again, this way does tell us something about God, if God exists at all. If perfection is beyond our grasp, then a full appreciation of God's perfection, and so God, will be too. The fourth way, like one and two, looks like another warning against idolatry.

Fifth comes the teleological argument. Nature is clearly harmonious, it states, a wonderfully intricate organic whole. Therefore it must have a purpose; there must be an end in mind for it. But whose mind? God. QED.

Rot! cries the sceptic. It is perfectly possible for something to have a purpose without anyone having designed it for that purpose. When I chew my pencil, I put it to a purpose that no one designed it for. Similarly, purpose needn't be in any being's mind, as the random processes of evolution that produce the intricacies of nature have demonstrably proven. And anyway, maybe it is we who see purpose and order in nature. The rationale for things could be in our minds, not that of any God.

That is all true. However, where and how people find purpose in life is a complex matter. It has to do with their sense of what it is to be a person; it arises from an embedded participation in life. Hence, for many, and in spite of the objections, there does, on balance, seem to be a creative, purposeful direction or energy subtly manifest in the course of the story of our cosmos, that emerges from the Big Bang and evolves our lives. That option may seem more plausible than the idea that the richness of life is due solely to the blind collisions of atoms. Even the blind collisions look to be 'about' something.

Darwinian delusions

It's also worth reconsidering the nature of Darwinian evolution. A new consensus is emerging as to how to interpret Darwin's great theory, and it is not one that automatically implies a directionless universe or godless cosmos.

In a way, you might say that atheistic Darwinism has overplayed its hand. The philosopher Daniel Dennett calls it a 'universal acid', by which he means that evolution can explain everything – not just why your ancestors had two legs or why they believed in a sky god, but why we think we have minds, ethics and free will too. They are all really delusions, the neo-Darwinian declares. They are extraordinarily useful survival adaptations, and that is why we live as if they were real, though they are not.

But is that plausible? As the theologian Conor Cunningham asks in a recent book, *Darwin's Pious Idea,* do neo-Darwinists practise what they preach? If they really thought that ethics was a delusion, wouldn't they cut not only the grass but their dogs; eat not only lettuce but their neighbour's children? Scratch an ultra-Darwinist, Cunningham suggests, and watch a hypocrite bleed. You don't mistake your wife, partner or husband for a person with a mind and free will. They *are* a person with a mind and free will.

> *You don't mistake your wife, partner or husband for a person with a mind and free will. They are a person with a mind and free will.*

Another line of readjustment concerns the possibility that evolutionary processes are not as blind as is usually asserted. Many features of organisms, from the sabre teeth of tigers to the proteins that function in cells, have been shown to have evolved many times over, and by completely separate paths. It is called convergence, and if it is right, it implies that there is a predictability to evolution. Nature keeps coming up with the same solutions. Consider that most demeaned of animals, the sloth, honoured by being named after one of the seven deadly sins. It turns out that these humble creatures come in two varieties. One has two toes, the other three. Further, the two species have completely separate evolutionary histories. That's fascinating. Is the humble sloth a piece of evidence that there might be directionality in evolution? It seems remarkable that random natural selection has come up at least twice with almost the same answer to hanging upside down in trees.

Such examples lead the theologian to ask whether God might be seen to be acting through evolution's apparent directionality. If that is the case, then why not accept that the world is somehow made right for the emergence of life like ours, life that is self-aware and God-seeking. Thomas Aquinas knew nothing about Darwinism, though he seems to have contemplated a possibility a little like it. 'It is clear', he wrote in the thirteenth century, 'that nature is a certain kind of divine art impressed upon things, by which these things are moved to a determinate end. It is as if a shipbuilder were able to give to timbers that by which they would move themselves to take the form of a ship.' Perhaps one day scientists will come to see that this is not a bad description of how evolution works.

It is a very controversial and speculative reading of evolution. But it is not ridiculous, and so it shouldn't be summarily dismissed. Aquinas's fifth way, teleology, may not be able to prove the existence of God, but it might show that belief in God is justifiable, given what we know about the world.

Mysterious God

Anselm's contribution comes in the form of the ontological argument, and posits simply and without apology that there is a God. But, asks the sceptic, what is this God like? Ah! replies the theist: the fundamental feature of God is existence. After all, something that exists must be greater than something that doesn't exist. So God must exist.

Whatever we might imagine God to be – a good God, a loving God, an all-powerful God, an all-knowing God – it is vital to remember that He is a mystery.

Rubbish, responds the sceptic. All you've done is insist that saying 'God is' proves that God is. And the vast majority of philosophers and theologians have concluded that on this one the sceptic is basically right – though, interestingly, they turn back repeatedly to Anselm's ontological argument. It has been around for quite a few centuries now, and yet has never died. Again, it throws up all manner of stimulating insights into the nature of being, existence and the issue we encountered before, necessity. The proof fails in a way, though in another, the issues it raises are revealing. What do they actually prove? you can ask. Well, if not God, then perhaps the fact that whatever we might imagine God to be – a good God, a loving God, an all-powerful God, an all-knowing God – it is vital to remember that He is a mystery. This is precisely what Aquinas concludes. All that we have fully proven, he says, is that the fundamental nature of divinity is mystery.

When it comes to theology, everything we might care to say will fall short. It works like this. Say we ascribe the quality of goodness to God, as people do, then what do we mean? If I describe my dinner as good, I know what I mean. It is tasty. But if I say God is good, I don't quite know what I mean, because God's goodness can't signify, say, divine tastiness.

But it is also the case that we frequently use words analogically and metaphorically, and life is so much the richer for it. Shakespeare has Macbeth muse, 'I have almost forgot the taste of fears.' He doesn't mean that Macbeth is about to pick up a fork to be reminded what fears taste like. He means something far more weighty. As Macbeth continues, 'I have supped full with horrors.' That's the kind of insight that metaphors allow us to reach for. They are more powerful for being expressed indirectly.

Or take the mystery that is the nature of the human mind. For all the ink that has been spilt, for all the brain scanners that have been booted up, the nature of mind becomes more elusive to us, not less. It is known as the hard problem, and people reach for all kinds of metaphors to discuss it. Mind is like a computer, they might say, which it is not, though the metaphor may contain something that is indirectly true about mind, and so is still worth saying.

And so it is with God, Aquinas concludes. Human beings are not divine. The 'proofs' prove that too. But the difference between the atheist and the believer is that where the atheist reads the 'proofs' and thinks: that just about does it for God, the believer admits: well, that's God for you. What else did you expect?

WILL SCIENCE PUT AN END TO RELIGION?

The politics of faith and the organization of unbelief

*B*uried in the sometimes calm, sometimes ferocious debate between science and religion, commentators have detected a variety of models about the relationship between the two. However, there is one that tends to grab most of the headlines. It is the conviction that science and religion are in conflict, a conflict that only one side can win.

Key players include the so-called new atheists, individuals such as biologist Richard Dawkins, who argue that pre-scientific, superstitious individuals strove to understand the universe using religious ideas. How was the world created? In six days, by the direct act of God. Why does lightning strike? It expresses the wrath of a deity and portends an ill future. What lies behind the extraordinary diversity of life in the world? The exuberant creative genius who has designed nature's intricacies to the astonishment and delight of all.

These atheists declare all such beliefs implausible, and as farcical as believing in the existence of fairies dancing around mushrooms behind the shed in your garden. The reason is that we now have science to deliver natural explanations that can account for all these phenomena. The world was 'created' out of the primordial fireball known as the Big Bang. Lightning strikes to release the build-up of electrostatic charge in the clouds. Nature's intricacies arise from the blind mechanisms of evolution by natural selection. The story of modern science is one of old religious explanations being usurped by new empirical ones: the true ones.

The model is conflictual because it is given the added twist of being a zero-sum game: scientific explanations can only progress in so far as the religious ones are ousted. Leave a gap for God, the argument goes, and you leave an opening for a regressive superstition that threatens the explanatory progress that has been made. By way of proof for their antagonistic attitude towards religions, individuals like Dawkins highlight one issue in particular: namely the rise of creationism in the USA and the demands to have it taught alongside evolution in the classroom.

> *Leave a gap for God, the argument goes, and you leave an opening for a regressive superstition that threatens the explanatory progress that has been made.*

It is true that a battle rages between some evolutionary scientists and the proponents of creationism and intelligent design. However, the question is whether it has been caused by the undoubtedly far-reaching insights of Charles Darwin, or provoked by a less subtle and more confrontational force: the rise of a certain kind of scientific attitude that readily picks fights with religion, and proponents of its mirror opposite, a religious sensibility that blames science for most of the woes of the modern world.

Fundamentalists versus intellectual freedom

A key moment came with the so-called 'Scopes monkey trial'. It was held in 1925, in Dayton, Tennessee, and concerned the teaching of evolution in state schools, something that had been made illegal. The governor had signed a decree forbidding 'any theory that denies the story of the Divine Creation of man as taught in the Bible, and to teach instead that man has descended from a lower order of animals'. Other states had taken note and seemed to be following suit: Mississippi and Arkansas turned against evolution too. The American Civil Liberties Union (ACLU) decided that it was time to defend intellectual freedom and champion the cause of evolution. John Scopes was the pro-evolution teacher who volunteered to put his career on the line; he was defended by the lawyer Clarence Darrow, a man who became famous largely as a result of the case.

That was partly because the prosecuting lawyer on the other side was William Jennings Bryan, a man who had stood for president – and lost – three times, though he was still a much-loved leader, known as 'The Great Commoner'. He championed the rights of downtrodden individuals and was a supporter of causes like votes for women.

The irony is that the case was clear. Legally speaking, conflict was not necessary. Scopes had broken the law, and sure enough he was found guilty and ordered to pay a fine. For decades afterwards evolution was not taught in schools. But the flames of conflict were fanned not so much by the specifics of the case as by everything else that was unleashed at the trial. Hence, Scopes has become as significant in sustaining the mythology of a struggle to the death between science and religion as has the trial of Galileo Galilei in the seventeenth century.

William Jennings Bryan, the anti-evolutionary lawyer, was a member of a new movement called the fundamentalists, a group that provides the name and original impetus for the more widespread fundamentalism we know today. The first fundamentalists saw themselves as defending the interests of common Christian folk, and did so by asserting a list of tenets deemed basic to Christianity. These were doctrinal lines in the sand that could not be crossed, and evolution crossed them mightily. Darwinism was thought not just unbiblical, but morally wrong. How could it be otherwise? the fundamentalists believed. The science that demoted human beings to descent from a 'lower order of animals' led to an ideology that fed the degeneration of society they were witnessing in their own day. As Bryan implored during his closing statement at the trial:

What shall we say of the intelligence, not to say religion, of those who are so particular to distinguish between fishes and reptiles and birds, but put a man with an immortal soul in the same circle with the wolf, the hyena and the skunk? What must be the impression made upon children by such a degradation of man?

Remember that this was the 1920s, a handful of years after the First World War and the Russian Revolution. The world was a fragile place, civilization was at risk, and some of the blame, fairly or not, was laid at Darwinism's door. Before the war, a relatively tolerant attitude towards evolution had existed amongst those who believed in the infallibility of the Bible. That largely disappeared during and afterwards, concludes Edward J. Larson in his seminal study of the trial, *Summer for the Gods: The Scopes Trial and America's Continuing Debate Over Science and Religion.*

On the other side, the pro-evolution American Civil Liberties Union had an agenda that was similarly deeply embedded in the troubled times. It was championing the cause of radical labour rights following the arrest and deportation of leftist activists deemed to be communist, Bolshevik and anarchic. In his book, Larson describes an ACLU composed of elitist, liberal New Yorkers 'who had grown wary of majoritarianism' – which is to say, wary of the common Christian folk that Bryan stood up for. 'Instinctively, they opposed popular movements to restrict academic freedom, such as the antievolution crusade', he continues; they also sought opportunities for direct action 'designed to enlighten public opinion'. The pro-evolutionists too felt that nothing less than the preservation of good moral order was at stake. The Scopes trial was, therefore, a perfect conflict and storm.

Then there is also the figure of Clarence Darrow in the eye of the vortex. He seized the trial stand to make a mockery of conservative Christian beliefs. It was not hard to do. Are Christians made of salt? he asked. After all, the Bible calls the followers of Jesus 'the salt of the earth'? No, of course not, his opponent, Bryan, replied. So was Jonah really swallowed by a whale? Darrow retorted. Yes, Bryan responded, pointing out that the Bible actually talks of a big fish rather than a whale. So if Eve was made out of Adam's rib, Darrow asked next, where did Cain's wife come from? Bryan had no idea.

The battering continued. Was the Bible right when it said that the Sun once stopped still in the sky? Yes, Bryan asserted: on that day, the Earth's rotation around its star froze. Was that Earth about 6,000 years old, as was commonly asserted in printed bibles that included marginalia setting the date of creation as 4004 BC? Bryan did not agree with that, and affirmed that the Earth was older, though by how much, he could not say. So what about the six days of creation? Darrow pressed. Were they 24-hour days? Bryan defended himself by calling them 'periods', noting that it was not important to faith how long they were.

Sourness permanently curdled the encounter. Eventually Darrow accused Bryan of having 'fool ideas that no intelligent Christian on earth believes'. To Bryan, the New York elitism of Darrow and the ACLU could not be more clearly manifest. It is a shame that the tone of the exchange is remembered more clearly than its content. The mood of the Tennessee courtroom has lingered so powerfully that it is not going too far to say that writers like Richard Dawkins, who are equally able to brilliantly explain science and pitilessly mock religion, are Darrow's rhetorical children.

Separating science and religion

Ever since the Scopes trial, the public presentation of evolution has been heavily politicized. Creationists of different sorts associate it with everything from militaristic government to homosexuality. Evangelical Darwinists link the advance of the biological sciences to matters from the health of the secular state to campaigns aimed at banning the burka. And the vitriol has not stopped at the borders of America. Inflamed concern about evolution has spread to countries with large Muslim populations too. A biologist who teaches at Cambridge University recently told me that he did not recall once hearing the word 'creationism' when he taught in Turkey during the 1970s. A few decades later, a Turkish anti-evolutionist who writes under the name of Harun Yayha has become so well funded that he recently sent copies of an expensive glossy book, illustrating so-called 'Creation Science', to every school in France.

The result is a near inability to discuss evolution in neutral terms. Again, this can be seen on both sides. A Jordanian biologist, Rana Dajani, told me that Darwin's works have only recently been translated into Arabic, so many young people have only had access to the popular, heated polemic. It is literally impossible for them to read the science without hearing antagonism in their ears, and so she has to spend much of her time demonstrating that evolution is not, in fact, incompatible with theological concepts in the Qur'an.

So the conflict model tends to dominate, though it is not the only one available. There are others to explore and, I'd suggest, adopt. They do not imply the end of religion with the rise of science. The battle is needless. They propose either that religion and science have nothing in common, or that one might even learn from the other.

> *Science and religion are two separate ways of looking at the world, each with their own excellence.*

The so-called 'two magisteria' model is a first non-conflictual possibility to consider. It is closely associated with the biologist Stephen Jay Gould, who wrote of the intellectual independence of science and religion. They are 'nonoverlapping magisteria', he wrote – magisteria being a Roman Catholic word defined as 'a domain where one form of teaching holds the appropriate tools for meaningful discourse and resolution'. Science and religion are two separate ways of looking at the world, each with their own excellence.

This model has a history too. It reaches back to the seventeenth century, when the view arose that there is a creator God, and that this divinity did little more than light the cosmic touchpaper before stepping back to watch His glorious creation unfold. This idea, known as deism, inculcated a belief, common amongst scientists to this day, that science and religion do best when they observe a respectful distance. Neither one can contribute meaningfully to the insights of the other, and when the lines between them are blurred, confusion is the most likely result. They simply work to different rules and deploy different apparatus, and in truth are as incompatible as football and rugby, in spite of any surface similarities.

This is nicely illustrated by a story concerning Pierre Laplace. A physicist, he improved upon inaccuracies in the celestial mechanics devised by Isaac Newton and wrote his ideas up in a book, *Système du monde*. Living in post-revolutionary France, he wisely took the precaution of presenting a copy to Napoleon. The leader commented that Laplace's genius was obvious. He was able to describe the workings of the heavens, only he had done so without reference to the universe's creator. 'I had no need of that hypothesis', Laplace retorted – to which Napoleon reportedly replied, 'But it is a fine hypothesis! It explains many things.' Not, though, in science.

Whatever the truth of the exchange, the detail to note is that Laplace was not an atheist. Neither was Newton. In fact, Laplace's chief hypothesis, that the solar system had evolved from a spiralling mass of incandescent gas, had been conceived of 60 years earlier by another Newtonian and Christian mystic, Emanuel Swedenborg. All that Laplace was insisting on was that nature is governed by mechanical principles, as he imagined the creator had decreed. God had prescribed them; He was not needed to describe them. Similarly, it seems that most scientists and many theologians hold to a practical separation of science and theology.

Isaac Newton and the Philosopher's Stone

The trouble with non-overlapping magisteria, though, is that it doesn't really work in practice. If Swedenborg inspired Laplace, Newton himself had been inspired by his own theological beliefs. In particular, he was an alchemist, writing a million words on the transmutation of metals and associated speculations concerning the spirit that lies locked up in matter. In the same way as an alchemist sought to release gold from lead, via identification with the Philosopher's Stone, so he also sought to release life from inert stuff. Newton aligned himself with Hermes Trismegistus, the mythical author of the mystical Hermetic Corpus. 'Yet I had this art and science by the sole inspiration of

ENGRAVING OF HERMES TRISMEGISTUS FROM *SYMBOLA AUREAE* (1617) BY MICHAEL MAIER. HERMES TRISMEGISTUS, THE THREE TIMES GREAT ONE, IS A MYTHICAL FIGURE, AND YET MANY IDEAS ASSOCIATED WITH HIM ARE EMBEDDED IN MODERN SCIENCE.

God who has vouchsafed to reveal it to his servant', he wrote in his copious notes. 'Who gives those that know how to use their reason the means of knowing the truth, but is never the cause that any man follows error & falsehood.'

The Hermetic Corpus inspired several of the principles that lie behind modern science. For example, Hermes Trismegistus encourages human beings not just to contemplate nature but to administer it, in order to perfect it. That requires the particular kind of understanding of nature that science seeks. It is a predictive and powerful, not just descriptive and beautiful, kind of knowledge.

The 'three times great one', as the name Trismegistus translates, also posits the universe itself to be alive, guided by a 'world-soul'. This had the effect of removing the need for the continuous intervention in the cosmos of an external God, to keep everything in motion, as the older Aristotelian view required. It is the deistic view of the universe as a self-contained, enclosed system, and is a philosophical prerequisite for science, which seeks signs of the laws of nature, not the hands of gods.

> *The deistic view of the universe as a self-contained, enclosed system is a philosophical prerequisite for science, which seeks signs of the laws of nature, not the hands of gods.*

In fact, once you start to look, theological insights are woven through modern science like a web. The idea that empirical research and repeated experiments constitute the only way to establish objective truth can be related back to the Christian conviction that the human mind is fallible because of the Fall. A number of people are needed to replicate experiments to overcome the inevitable flaws of any one individual. With the same Christian background, the scientist Robert Hooke was inspired by science's promise of regaining knowledge of the world as Adam had once known it in Eden.

A clash of cultures

Modern historical research has shown that in the critical periods of the sixteenth and seventeenth centuries, when science as we know it today really took root, almost two-thirds of the most important figures were not just Christian in a nominal sense, but exceptionally devout.

The irony is that the excessive piety of these scientists probably helped seed the modern problem. The historian of religion Steven Shapin has argued in his book *The Scientific Revolution* that a crucial phase of the revolution – if that is what it was – occurred in the nineteenth century. It was more of an ideological than an empirical revolt.

Before this period, science had been dominated by clergymen and amateurs. But in the nineteenth century, it became professionalized. The country parson catching butterflies in his vicarage garden was out. The word 'scientist' itself was invented in the 1870s, and began to carry anticlerical connotations. They were stirred up by individuals such as T.H. Huxley, the founder of the X Club, a society devoted to science, 'pure and free, untrammelled by religious dogmas', as one member wrote to Charles Darwin in 1865. Huxley nurtured this new mood amongst his followers:

> *Extinguished theologians lie about the cradle of every science as the strangled snakes beside that of Hercules; and history records that whenever science and orthodoxy have been fairly opposed, the latter has been forced to retire from the lists, bleeding and crushed if not annihilated; scotched, if not slain.*

We're back to conflict again. That was when the outlines emerged of what we now see as a clash of scientific and religious cultures, as well as the familiar debating points used to 'show' that science trumps religion. The pre-scientific and superstitious thought that the world was flat, it might now be said, might seem convincing until you wonder why Christopher Columbus in the fifteenth century did not have to reassure his sailors that they wouldn't slip off the edge of the world. Or there is the belief that the history of science is scattered with martyrs who were burnt at the stake merely for following the evidence, when the truth is that science has only one martyr. It was not Galileo, who suffered house arrest when he crossed the Pope, and whose fate was really a product of their two antagonistic characters and the niceties of Catholic theology, not of whether the earth moves. The one actual martyr was poor Giordano Bruno, and he probably met a fiery, brutal end because of his belligerent advocacy of occult, rather than scientific, beliefs. You might say that superstition was responsible for science's one martyr. There's an irony in that too.

So the conflict between science and religion is not inevitable. It is relatively recent and primarily political. The answer to our question – does the rise of science mean the end of religion? – is clearly no.

But we've also seen how trying to separate science from religion is not plausible either. The attempt to establish clear water between the two can only be achieved at the price of muddying both the history of science and the philosophy that underpins it. What, then, is an appropriate model for the relationship between the two? An answer awaits our next question.

WHY DO PEOPLE STILL HAVE RELIGIOUS BELIEFS?

How science generates wonder and how stones might speak

G od Is Back declares the title of a recent book by two writers at the Economist. *Even better, John Micklethwait and Adrian Wooldridge continue, He never went away. It was only in certain corners of north-western Europe that religious belief appeared to be in decline. In China, in South America, in Africa, in Russia, in North America, in the Middle East, faith communities prosper.*

The survival of religion

The World Religion Database captures the big statistic. The twentieth century was, in a way, one hundred years of argument in favour of atheism. There were hideous wars and the horrors of camps and gulags. That should undermine the notion that a deity created the world and saw that it was good. Or you could highlight the development of sophisticated philosophies championing atheism, such as those of Karl Marx. Marx argued that religion wouldn't be defeated by logic but would simply fade away as people's material needs were increasingly successfully met. Many people's material needs have indeed been fulfilled in a way unprecedented in history, and yet, the World Religion Database records, only around 2 per cent of global populations are atheists. At least three-quarters of the human race identify with a theistic belief. The vast majority of people in the world believe in God or gods. Thus it ever was. And thus it appears it will always be too.

> *The twentieth century was, in a way, one hundred years of argument in favour of atheism.*

Just why *Homo religiosus* survives is our question here, and by way of getting at it, it is worth adding a few more details to this initial background picture, not least because God's persistence has caught many commentators by surprise. 'The resurgence of religion was not foreseen', writes Harvey Cox in his book *The Future of Faith*. Cox, one of the key sociologists of religion, had argued the opposite:

> *On the contrary, not many decades ago thoughtful writers were confidently predicting its imminent demise. Science, literacy, and more education would soon dispel the miasma of superstition and obscurantism. Religion would either disappear completely or survive in family rituals, quaint folk festivals, and exotic references in literature, art, and music.*

So why has this not happened?

We need to consider again the issue of the relationship between science and religion. We've already had a first stab at it in the previous chapter. I concluded that science does not trump theology, though we were left with the question of just how to model the relationship between these two great modes of understanding. Another possibility presents itself now, which has to do with what might be called a 'God-shaped hole', and which sheds light on what is currently happening in the marketplace of religious belief.

Evidence and perception

This model is based on complementarity, and unsettles those who like the tidy distinctions implied by the notion that science and religion are two separate things. It also irritates those wedded to the belief that the rise of science means the fall of religion. But it can be unpacked in a true story – the story of how the great eighteenth-century German polymath Johann Wolfgang von Goethe became embroiled in the apparently trivial question of whether or not human beings have an intermaxillary bone.

Animals had long been known to possess this anatomical feature in their jaws. But the great anatomist of Goethe's time,

31

Petrus Camper, denied that human beings had one – which was just as well, he thought, as its absence demonstrated with hard physiology that there were tangible differences between human beings and animals. With no intermaxillary bone, humanity's unique position in creation could be held secure.

Goethe had a different idea. He carefully studied a number of human and animal skulls, and by 'reflection and coincidence', as he put it, showed that humans do indeed have an intermaxillary bone, though it lies hidden, like a shadow, in the upper jaw.

Camper refused to be persuaded, a denial that convinced Goethe that science is shaped by how scientists subjectively see the world, as well as by the objective evidence they provide in support of their perceptions. He reflected: 'One cannot convince a master of his error because [the unseen error] was taken as an integral part of the system which made him a master and thereby legitimized [him].' When new evidence challenges the original perception, it is likely to be resisted by reinterpretation or outright hostility, particularly when reputations are at stake. In a later letter to a friend, Goethe phrased it even more strongly: 'I would not put it past a scholar by profession to deny his five senses. These people are rarely concerned with real living ideas of things, but with what has been said of them.'

> *Scientists must be aware that how they look at the world as creatures of flesh and blood, emotion and imagination, matters as much as how they try to look at it as objective scientists.*

Goethe was not against science, though. Far from it. He devoted much of his efforts to its advance. Rather, he argued that scientists must be aware that how they look at the world as creatures of flesh and blood, emotion and imagination, matters as much as how they try to look at it as objective scientists. The apparently cool detachment of the laboratory is deluding. Rather than trying to achieve a system of observation that effectively denies that scientists are human beings, it would be better to achieve a system that optimizes a synthesis of reason and intuition, of thinking and feeling. After all, are not these the faculties that the scientist brings to the laboratory bench anyway?

Dialogue and integration

In time, the existence of the human intermaxillary bone was accepted, and proved to be no trivial discovery too. It inspired the concept of homology, the study of similar characteristics across different species, something that was much used by Darwin. Goethe himself did not explain such characteristics as the result of common ancestry, as the theory of evolution was to demonstrate seventy or so years later. Instead, he saw them as evidence of an underlying archetype of which features like bones are visible manifestations. This physiological blueprint is not itself visible. It can only be inferred indirectly by observation, portrayed 'if not to the sense then at any rate to the mind', as he put it. It is an approach to science based as much on reflection as scrutiny.

Hence Goethe could look at the hoof of a horse and 'see' the residual five fingers therein. He deployed the notion most strikingly in relation to plants, developing the concept of the *Urpflanze*. This is the archetypal shape and morphology of a plant – the roots that mirror the branches, the leaves whose structures mirror both. 'Nature proceeds from ideas, just as man follows an idea in all he undertakes', he summarized.

But that seemed to be going too far for a strictly empirical science. It overplays the role of imagination and feeling, speaking as if nature itself has those two attributes. Post-Darwinian orthodoxy is that nature does not proceed from ideas, as if it has a design. Instead it is shaped by the lesser goal of purpose, also called the survival of the fittest. And in fact, some of Goethe's speculative conjectures were subsequently shown to be wrong.

A well-known case is that of teeth and horns. Goethe presumed that animals that have large canine teeth, like cats, cannot have horns, like cows. This is because, according to his theory, large teeth and horns correspond to one another. The archetype means that an animal can have one or the other, but not both. Subsequent fossil evidence, not available to him, has revealed the existence of animals that indeed have had both.

Nonetheless there is surely something in Goethe's desire to establish an integrative model of science. If the aim is to find a complementary relationship between science and religion, there are reasons to pay attention to him still.

Humanity is nourished by its connection with nature, those links providing spiritual sustenance too, because in contemplating them, human beings become sensible of the patterns and harmonies that run through all things.

For one thing, Goethe's delight in his discovery of the intermaxillary bone runs contrary to the dismay religious creationists today show towards evolution. He was convinced that being part of nature, as the bone implies, is not a demotion or a degradation of human dignity. Being an animal does not imply being morally degenerate, as if humans can behave no better than apes. Instead, it welcomes and validates the extraordinary enjoyment and inspiration that human beings can find in nature. 'Nature is so kind and good', he wrote in one poem. He felt this sensuous corporality feeding him as a mother feeds her child at the breast. Humanity is nourished by its connection with nature, those links providing spiritual sustenance too, because in contemplating them, human beings become sensible of the patterns and harmonies that run through all things. Unlike the religious creationist, who would force a split between the material and the spiritual, Goethe integrates both elements as a resource to feed the human, body and soul.

Similarly, he seeks to dissolve any neat distinctions between science and religion, between contemplation and investigation, between a mechanical take on nature and viewing the cosmos as alive. His is a complementary model of the relationship between science and religion that is one of dialogue and integration.

By way of example, consider the meditative essay written by Annie Dillard, entitled *Teaching a Stone to Talk*. (I do not know whether Dillard reads Goethe, though it is striking that Goethe began a work entitled *A Novel: The Universe*, the only remaining part of which is focused on the 'most unshakeable son of nature', granite.) Dillard begins by confessing that she knows a man called Larry who is trying to instruct sand to speak. It is a seemingly mad enterprise, until, that is, you ask what the whole scientific enterprise is secretly about. Is it not trying to do the same: to recover a lost sense of connection with the cosmos?

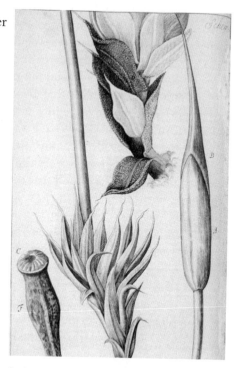

A DRAWING OF MOSS FROM *MICROGRAPHIA* BY ROBERT HOOKE. THESE DRAWINGS APPEAR BEAUTIFUL NOT JUST BECAUSE THEY ARE ACCURATE BUT BECAUSE THEY LET NATURE SPEAK.

Dillard notes that, as human subjects, science asks us to see ourselves as distant from nature, as objective observers of it. Physics does not see the vivid shades of the colour red, as we do, but rather electromagnetic radiation of about 650nm wavelength. Meteorologists do not admit to hearing the wind's cry, as a poet might; instead they measure its speed. Geologists do not publicly catch a mountain shouting praise, as the psalmist did; they drily report its age. But does that mean that nature is really silent, Dillard asks, or simply that science has encouraged us to develop the habit of not paying attention to this aspect of it? We study it, for sure, and what is discovered is marvellous. But do we seriously listen to it? Is Larry's talking stone a 'show we drove from town'?

She implies that it is, and, like Goethe, raises the prospect of a kind of science that does not, in fact, need to destroy 'the poetry of the rainbow, by reducing it to the prismatic colours', as Keats feared – and as Goethe had tried to resist too, in fact, with his own dynamic theory of colour. 'What have we been doing all these centuries but trying to call God back to the mountain, or, failing that, raise a peep out of anything that isn't us?' Dillard asks hopefully at the end of her essay. She goes a step further, enquiring: 'What is the difference between a cathedral and a physics lab? Are they not both saying: Hello?' This would be the kind of science that animates nature for us, as opposed to portraying it as a blind machine.

A God-shaped hole

In fact, this more complementary way of presenting science is often found in the genre of popular science. Take *The Cloudspotter's Guide* by Gavin Pretor-Pinney. Its extraordinary success must rest in no small part on the imaginative efforts to which the author goes to help our minds 'reach for the clouds'. Alongside explanations of the science, references to the gods are scattered throughout his meditation, not just because people used to believe that divinities sat on thrones of cumulus clouds, but because theological metaphors speak to us still. Think of the shafts of sunlight that radiate down from the heavens, Pretor-Pinney invites us: 'Sometimes they shine down through a hole in a thick cloud layer – of Stratocumulus, perhaps – like the gaze of some unseen god, made visible by the vapours.'

Another recent case in point concerns the hugely popular British TV series *Wonders of the Universe*, presented by Brian Cox. It was typical of this kind of science communication, featuring graphics and images of deep space and exploding nebulae set to the rising swell and celebratory trumpets of orchestral music. However, as it turned out, the programme-makers received a number of complaints that the musical accompaniment to the pictures was too loud. Viewers could not hear the science Cox was explaining, as he gazed wistfully heavenwards.

I thought the complaints were revealing. For it is surely the music rather than the strict science that speaks more loudly of the wonder we find in modern cosmology. It is true that we are made of carbon and carbon is made in stars, so we are stardust. But describing the carbon cycle at the heart of the nuclear reactions buried deep beneath the corona is not that inspiring. Rather, it is crescendos and choruses that truly communicate to us the meaning of the stark scientific fact. Science needs music. It helps human beings to interpret the physics, and thereby to place it imaginatively in the context of our lives. The programme made raids on the language of values and metaphysics to convey its message of cosmological enlightenment. It needed the beauty of colour and rich harmonies – qualities that, of themselves, again are unknown to physics as physics. It deployed a complementary model between science and spiritual sensibilities.

What this all adds up to is evidence that human beings have a God-shaped hole, or at least that many of us are naturally, spontaneously spiritual in our sentiments. What is science if not a generator of the biggest of big questions. Where do we come from? Where are we going? And these are religious questions too. The one kind of answer complements the other. The science reminds us that we have a desire for the infinite, as Aristotle put it, felt when we gaze at images of interstellar space. And we can reach for the infinite in our spiritual questing too. The story of how we are made of carbon created in stars addresses the restless heart that longs to know where it belongs. And this is the same restless heart that St Augustine, for one, believed finds its fullest satisfaction when 'tilted' towards the divine. We can conclude that *Homo religiosus* survives because science does not remove or fill in the God-shaped hole. Actually, it makes us more aware of the meaning dimension.

> Homo religiosus *survives because science does not remove or fill in the God-shaped hole.*

'All theory, dear friend, is grey', wrote Goethe to a friend. 'But the golden tree of actual life springs ever green.' The spiritual imagination can be fed by modern science, and in science, human beings have discovered an excellent way to feed it.

IS RELIGION A MISTAKE OF EVOLUTION?

Cave art and whether brains make meaning or find it

*B*elief in deities must have evolved. But evolutionary accounts of religion often smuggle in unwarranted assumptions too, such as that faith is misguided, a hangover from more primitive times. Is that right? Let us wind the clock back to those so-called primitive times.

Caverns of the mind

Aurignac is a modest, attractive town in the south-west of France. The clay-tiled roofs of its houses seem to crowd up the hillside, and are topped by a single round turret, the remains of a medieval castle. Climb up and you are rewarded with the snow-topped expanse of the Pyrenees mountains stretching across the southern horizon.

If you drive west from the town, you pass signs for some local caves. They too are modest when set alongside some of the other complexes you can visit in the region. However, the caves of Aurignac had the good fortune to be discovered by Edouard Lartet in 1860. In them, he found the remnants of a prehistoric human culture now famous for its cave art and known as Aurignacian.

These people probably arrived in Europe around 40,000 years ago. The remains in Aurignac and elsewhere testify to an explosion in tool-making, including the invention of the burin, a pointed instrument that makes a very effective engraver. It was essential for the art.

THE PAINTINGS OF PREHISTORIC MAN, SUCH AS THOSE AT LASCAUX, MAY CAPTURE A CRITICAL MOMENT WHEN OUR ANCESTORS REALIZED THAT THEY WERE BOTH LIKE AND UNLIKE OTHER ANIMALS.

The paintings and reliefs that cover the walls and ceilings of limestone caves dotted around southern France are mostly of animals, remarkably naturalistic in style, though with subtle twists and repetitions that cleverly create a sense of movement and dynamism too. Horses and bulls. Lions and gazelles. Panthers and bears. Occasionally you can see the fecund form of a female human being, or the palm and five fingers of a human hand, made by blowing paint across it as if using a stencil. They are impressive, in polychrome colours of red, brown, yellow and black; a memory of human souls that echoes across the centuries.

The most famous caves are at Lascaux. When Picasso visited them, he remarked that art had learned nothing since. Our scribblings and compositions are but footnotes. It is doubly remarkable that these works appear to have suddenly arrived in Europe almost perfectly formed. Little wonder that they have a power both immediate and accessible. The art still speaks across the millennia. It makes you wonder how much of the art of our times will prove so durable.

Recently a new complex was discovered, at Chauvet. It has been sealed from the public, as a result of the lessons learnt at Lascaux: the images there faded fast because of the breath of the crowds that pressed into its subterranean spaces. Instead, the Chauvet cave has been filmed by Werner Herzog, and presented to the public in his 3-D film *Cave of Forgotten Dreams*.

One of the archaeologists in the film well captures the experience of being in the caves. He reports working underground for about five days, being very close to the images, in their presence, and then realizing that he needed to take time out. He was working as a scientist, but the paintings had an effect on him as a human being. He had been having dreams, he reported, of lions. They weren't frightening. Rather, they seemed to transmit a meaning that was deep and profound, of a reality beyond direct representation.

Another rock painting expert in the film, who had worked on the art of Australian Aborigines, told the story of a scientist who was travelling to a site with an Aborigine guide. When they arrived, the paintings were damaged and the guide, quite spontaneously, began to touch them up. The scientist objected, for fear of losing evidence, and the guide gave a wonderful reply. I am not doing the painting, he said. It is the spirit, the dreaming.

The modern century's term for it is the unconscious, those caverns of the mind that are forever excluded from the daylight of consciousness, though when they are tapped they release the energy of horses and lions into our lives. Aurignacian man was not just a good artist. At that moment in our evolution, he glimpsed the truth – perhaps for the first time – that life is more than just a struggle for survival. It has meaning. The fruits of the chase don't just feed his body. They also clothe his soul.

Superstitious man

As the millennia passed, prehistoric art developed in finery. Another outstanding piece to survive, now in the British Museum in London, depicts swimming reindeer. Made out of a single mammoth tusk, so that the beasts appear to traverse along its length, it was found in a town not far from Aurignac. It featured in the BBC radio series *A History of the World in 100 Objects*, during which Rowan Williams, the Archbishop of Canterbury, offered some reflections on its religious significance. He described how it speaks to him of the human desire to be at home in the world at a deep level, a common religious impulse.

> *Life is more than just a struggle for survival. It has meaning.*

> *You can feel that somebody's making this who was projecting themselves with huge imaginative generosity into the world around, and saw and felt in their bones that rhythm. In the art of this period you see human beings trying to enter fully into the flow of life, so that they become part of the whole process of animal life that's going on around them.*

Ancient stone circles can provoke a similar sense of being a citizen of the cosmos. I remember visiting the Rollright Stones on the border of Oxfordshire and Warwickshire. Standing in the middle of the megaliths, which are around human height, made me realize that when you are in a circle, there is nowhere to hide. That creates a sense of presence and focus. It is as if the circle intensifies the experience of life, acting like a magnifying lens for the spiritual emotions. There is a minor shift in dimension, as if cutting through the surface to the hidden, to a core of being. Like the cave paintings, stone circles may be prehistoric, but they are timeless in their power and impact.

I dwell on this ancient art and artefacts because a common assumption made about religious beliefs and feelings today is that they are primitive. It is as if myth and ritual are the remnants of more basic and superstitious times that should be shed now that we are more scientific and rational – though I suspect that this says more about the imaginative limitations of those who advocate such views than it does about the religious experience of our forebears. For like Picasso, many of those who encounter this art suspect that its symbolism and perception of things is as advanced and sophisticated as the greatest works that have been created since.

Citizens of the cosmos

Such a derogatory assumption is worth bearing in mind, particularly when reading about the evolutionary origins of religion. There is a powerful desire in our culture to explain each and every facet of what it is to be human by the light of Darwin's great insights. Religion is no exception, and the dominant account rests on the idea that spiritual convictions are basically a mistake, if one that helped to secure survival advantage. It tells a story that goes something like this.

> *There is a powerful desire in our culture to explain each and every facet of what it is to be human by the light of Darwin's great insights.*

Think of our ancestors again, struggling to stay alive. It was tough. Around every rock, within each thicket, lurked threats. Life had a single rule, kill or be killed, and so our increasingly smart forebears learnt to exploit their intelligence to detect and outwit their enemies.

But matters got out of control. Human intelligence generates, as a by-product, tremendous powers of imagination. And imagination can run riot. A rustling shrub might contain a deadly snake, or maybe the shifting leaves are a sign of something else that is out to get us – a demon, perhaps, or a goblin. As a result, people became animists, believing that winds and stones, beasts and echoes were inhabited by spirits. *Homo sapiens* grew wildly superstitious. He couldn't help it. As the evolutionary psychologist Jesse Bering explains in his book *The God Instinct*, 'we sometimes can't help but see intentions, desires, and beliefs in things that haven't even a smidgeon of a neural system there to generate the psychological states we perceive'. But though fantastical, this capacity aided our survival. Better to be fooled and not killed when the rustle is a snake, than relaxed about cracks and swishes and eaten when the threat turns out to be real.

More technically, this story of adaptive advantage is known as 'domain violation'. The theory is that the human brain first evolved by developing specialist units or domains. It was like a smartphone, with an app for language, an app for empathy, an app for sex, an app for prediction. However, sometimes different apps interfered with one another. The app for empathy, say, might overrun the app for prediction and, as a result, empathically intuit that the sunrise each day is actually a sign of the favour of the sun god Helios. This app or domain violation produces sun worship. But it is a mistake. The sun is not worthy of worship. It will rise tomorrow regardless of our feelings towards it. And yet we can't but help feel thankful for the sunrise. The sense that the cosmos is somehow 'for us' might have helped us stay positive and so alive, in spite of all of the ills with which life presents us. It was useful. That's why it became part of our mythology. Indeed, we still worship the sun, in every holiday trip to the beach. That's the legacy of primitive beliefs for you. They linger on.

The theory is supported by lots of circumstantial evidence. Some of the most interesting examines the way in which we use language. Various experiments show that we tend to be drawn to images and ideas that convert literal signifiers into metaphorical meanings. The Bible tells of donkeys that speak. Myths describe carpets that fly. In ancient tales, spirits appear in whirlwinds. In animated movies there are toys that come to the rescue. The oddness of these associations – which the anthropologist Pascal Boyer calls 'minimally counterintuitive' – means that they lodge in our memory and we are inclined to deploy them, partly out of amusement, partly out of the ancient intuition, or hope, that life has a deeper meaning.

This leads to a never-ending play of stories and speculations on religious themes. Believers interpret this play as the struggle to picture and express hidden truths, truths that will ultimately remain beyond us because we are mortals trying to grasp the immortal; we are finite creatures yearning for the infinite. However, the evolutionary theory suggests that the play is, in fact, empty. It is the product of domain violation, an overactive imagination, the tendency to see evil in the hollows of trees, and has as much bearing on reality as the signs of the zodiac do on the scattering of stars in the galaxy.

If true, this is clearly damaging to religion. It is, indeed, an evolutionary mistake. But is the theory plausible, let alone right? What if we are not inclined to see spirits lurking in every dark corner, or if domain violation is not a misfiring brain but is actually the way that cognition works?

The holistic brain

For one thing, I suspect that our ancestors were not as jumpy and stressed as the evolutionary picture implies. Observe other animals today. Do dogs snarl and cats arch their backs every time there is a knock or scratch from another room in the house? Sometimes an ear is raised. Sometimes the animal sits up. Occasionally they do growl and move to the door to investigate. But mostly they sleep on. If these animals are capable of discerning the difference between background noise and real threat, surely our ancestors were often able to do so too. They could learn when to relax, when to be on guard.

There is evidence that we develop the capacity for such discernment as we grow up. Another psychologist, Justin Barrett, has researched the way young children form beliefs in gods. He concludes that human beings are inclined to be theological. For example, as children we probably tend to assume that the world around us is designed, and designed with us in mind. 'For instance', Barrett writes in a paper entitled 'Cognitive Science of Religion: What Is It and Why Is It?', 'children are inclined to say rocks are "pointy" not because of some physical processes but because being pointy keeps them from being sat upon.'

Later on though, children develop the ability to make distinctions between humans and gods. A child will then trust that there are some things his parents don't know, but that God does, such as his secret thoughts. Or they might learn to rely on benign forces when they realize that their parents won't be there to help them, such as during the dark hours of the night. So if children by about the age of five can tell the difference between the human and divine, then surely our adult forebears would have known that there can be a difference between the snap of a twig caused by a lion's paw and the snap of a twig caused by a gust of wind. 'Hyperactive agency detection', as it is called, is less plausible than the story about the dangers of life on the savannah might lead us to suppose.

There is another view of the brain's involvement in this development that also challenges the theory of domain violation too. Two more psychologists, Philip Barnard and Fraser Watts, argue that whilst some brain functions do seem to be modular, other functions that are possibly more fundamental always involve the whole brain and are not domain-specific. This would mean that the notion of domain violation, and the supposed erroneous beliefs that follow from it, is flawed in its conception.

A holistic, rather than modular, capacity served humanity particularly well when it came to the cultural explosion marked by the emergence of Aurignacian culture, the archaeology that shows our ancestors starting to bury their dead, devise sophisticated tools and paint on the walls of caves. What enabled this dramatic cognitive shift away from our nearest evolutionary relatives was the 'fluid intelligence' that could not arise if our brains were basically like smartphones, with discrete applications developed for this and that. If you think about it, this makes good sense. A smartphone is not smart in itself. It is only smart when it is used by smart people who know how to utilize its disconnected functionality with seamless fluidity as they navigate a path through the many tasks of life.

This suggests that culture and religion explode on the scene because when the human brain reaches a certain point of development, human

The misfiring brain does not generate the fantasies of religion. It is a wonderfully honed tool for discerning the meaning to be found in creation.

beings are relatively quickly able to take a massive leap in their understanding of the world as the world actually is. The misfiring brain does not generate the fantasies of religion. It is a wonderfully honed tool for discerning the meaning to be found in creation. Aurignacian culture is part of that discovery, as are the swimming reindeer that express how people felt at home in the world and integral to the flow of life.

Seeking meaning in the universe

Over time, these first experiments led to other forms of intelligent exploration, such as the development of geometry and mathematics, aspects of culture that many people would quite naturally assume are not the product of mere play, but rather means of capturing and representing the cosmos as it actually is. Science is not an evolutionary mistake. It's progress. So why not religious exploration too?

Again, language provides evidence, this time in support of the new hypothesis. Instead of examining the way in which we use language now, a different approach treats languages like a fossil record of our intellectual prehistory. Watts points to ancient words like the Hebrew '*ruach*', meaning both breath and spirit, or to words like 'light' that can simultaneously take on literal and metaphorical meanings: there is the 'light of day' and the 'light of reason'.

> *Science is not an evolutionary mistake. It's progress. So why not religious exploration too?*

The implication is that the literal did not come first, only later to become misleadingly metaphorical. Both modes emerge together. Further, the work of psychologist Solomon Asch shows that the same double-aspect meanings are found to exist in many different languages that are not historically linked. That may be the result of an extraordinary coincidence in the empty games played with words. Or it may be because of a profound intuition that breath and spirit are both elements necessary for life, to highlight the one example. It is like the chase depicted on the cave wall: it feeds body and soul together.

There is a further twist in this different story provided by the evolutionary paleobiologist Simon Conway Morris. He too has studied the emergence of cognitive systems like the brain. His idea is that just as lungs exploit the niche in the environment that we call the atmosphere, and gills exploit the niche in the environment that we call the seas, perhaps the brain exploits a less tangible but no less real niche in the environment that might be called the mental sphere. We have the kind of brain we do, as well as the cultural and religious manifestations with which it is bound up, because there is a cosmos out there to explore in terms of meaning as well as in terms of survival. We are not meaning-making creatures, but meaning-seeking creatures.

These ideas are all speculative, on both sides of the debate. And evolution does challenge many religious traditions in several respects. In a way, that is only to be expected. Darwin unleashed a new explanatory scheme, the power and limits of which we are still exploring and developing. I suspect that the most profound question it poses for believers is why a creator God would deploy such an extraordinarily long-winded, wasteful and painful means of making the world. Perhaps that is the price that must be paid for a creation that is also astonishingly beautiful. Maybe the aeons of time it takes are an expression of divine exuberance. After all, a thousand years in our sight are like a single watch in the night for God, as the psalmist remembers.

The evolutionary debate about religion is only just getting going. It is far too early to conclude that belief is an evolutionary mistake. 'Though the evolutionary approach to religion is currently intertwined with atheism, I suggest that evolutionary data are compatible with a much more positive view of religion than is normally imagined', Fraser Watts explained in a talk entitled 'Darwin's Gifts to Theology', given in September 2007 to the the 'Science and Religion Forum' of the University of Cambridge. 'Though these are early days in the evolutionary approach to religion, it is an approach that may yet enrich our understanding of the nature of religion in ways that are constructive and helpful.'

CAN DRUGS INDUCE RELIGIOUS EXPERIENCES?

The oldest spiritual practice, mysticism and the wonder of perception

*G*ood trip? For millennia, human beings have used drugs to *educe mystical illumination. Imbibing psychedelics has been called the oldest form of spiritual practice. Wise shamans were the carriers of generations of insight in how to use entheogens, 'creators of the god within'. With lengthy preparations they would guide novices towards the cosmic wonders that might be disclosed. So it is odd that in the modern world, drugs are often cited not to authenticate religious experience but to debunk it.*

The power of drugs apparently to cause religious experiences, and thereby explain them, is employed to question a wide variety of sacred insight. The prophet Moses, who encountered Yahweh in the Burning Bush, did not see a miracle, it has been suggested. Rather, he was high on a naturally growing psychedelic brew called ayahuasca. He was not close to some supposed deity, just stoned – lending a whole new meaning to the story that the mountain became enveloped in a 'cloud of smoke'.

> *Religion is not the opiate of the people, it is the by-product of opiates. Drugs make us susceptible to superstitious thinking.*

Or there is the prophetess who spoke for the god Apollo as the oracle of Delphi. She is said to have inhaled hallucinogenic vapours naturally emitted from the rocks on which the temple was built. In fact, the latest research suggests that the strata could never have emitted gases. They are not the right kind of rocks. But that hasn't stopped sceptics from mocking the mysteries of the oracle as a drug-induced high.

In short, religion is not the opiate of the people, it is the by-product of opiates. Drugs make us susceptible to superstitious thinking. No wonder the shamans employed them.

AN ATHENIAN RED-FIGURE KYLIX (DRINKING CUP) DEPICTING THE DELPHIC ORACLE, SITTING ON HER TRIPOD, BEING CONSULTED BY AEGEUS, KING OF ATHENS.

A related theory is that religious experiences are caused by temporal lobe epilepsy. This possibility has been explored via the so-called 'God Helmet', a motorcycle hat wired with electromagnets so as to cause microseizures. Subjects often report strange presences in the laboratory room, or feeling as if they are out of their bodies, or having psychic experiences. The explanation offered is that the electromagnets cause 'interhemispheric intrusions'. The left hemisphere of the brain, which usually dominates, is temporally overwhelmed by the right, leading to various fantastical disturbances in the sense of self. These can, in turn, be interpreted as of spiritual significance.

Whether the helmet stimulates such altered states of consciousness has been contested by other scientists in the field who have tried to replicate the experiments. But that challenge has not stopped reporting in the media, with the resulting assumption that religious experiences might be nothing more than a side effect of a brain malfunction.

Insights into reality

There is little doubt that entheogens do lead people to
experiences that convey a sense of being part of something bigger.
They can also help people to face fears and overcome them. Or
they can just expose them to terrors and fears. Aldous Huxley
took mescaline in the 1950s and as a result wrote a book, *The
Doors of Perception*, in which he explains:

> *The man who comes back through the Door in the Wall will never
> be quite the same as the man who went out. He will be wiser but
> less sure, happier but less self-satisfied, humbler in acknowledging
> his ignorance yet better equipped to understand the relationship
> of words to things, of systematic reasoning to the unfathomable
> mystery which it tries, forever vainly, to comprehend.*

The title of his book comes from a line of William Blake,
the poet, artist and mystic: 'If the doors of perception were
cleansed every thing would appear to man as it is, infinite. For
man has closed himself up, till he sees all things through narrow
chinks of his cavern.'

So the question is not whether highs can feel spiritual.
Rather, it is whether spiritual highs can, at least sometimes, be
regarded as authentic. Do they help convey true insights into
the nature of reality? Can they assist in catching sight of God? I
suspect that the answer is that they can, properly discerned. Some
hallucinogenics might aid not delusions, but openings in the
chinks of the cavern. In order to understand why this might be
a possibility, two prior questions need to be asked. First, what are
mystical experiences like? Second, are ordinary experiences so
different from them?

William James, the psychologist of religion, asked the
first question in his seminal lectures, subsequently published
as *The Varieties of Religious Experience*. He agreed that 'personal
religious experience has its root and centre in mystical states of
consciousness'. He also insisted that while the words 'mystical' and
'mysticism' can be used in a derogatory sense – as if they have no

basis in fact or logic – that does not preclude experiences that are meaningful. In fact, religious experiences tend to be regarded as carrying a knowledge and authority that is out of reach of discursive, rational thought.

This is because such weighty occurrences are felt more than they are thought; they are undergone rather than planned. They have the quality of ineffability, being beyond words. Again, this need not be put down to deliberate obfuscation and an indulgent fuzziness, for many common human experiences are difficult to describe, and are no less significant and real. 'One must have musical ears to know the value of a symphony; one must have been in love one's self to understand a lover's state of mind', according to James. 'Lacking the heart or ear, we cannot interpret the musician or the lover justly, and are even likely to consider him weak-minded or absurd.'

> *Religious experiences tend to be regarded as carrying a knowledge and authority that is out of reach of discursive, rational thought.*

Another feature of mystical states is that they are limited in duration, though for the individual who takes them seriously they can have a lasting impact upon everyday life. 'They modify the inner life of the subject between the times of their recurrence', James explains – a typical kind of modification being seeing the familiar and humdrum as weighty and significant. A phrase or place that was once thought unremarkable suddenly seizes the attention and claims centre stage. It is understood.

The ordinary becomes extraordinary

Owen Barfield, the philologist and friend of J.R.R. Tolkien and C.S. Lewis, recalls how the poetry of writers like William Wordsworth, which had been familiar to him since school, began to take on a new intensity at about the age of 21. His experience is a case of what William James highlights in his analysis: the ordinary becomes extraordinary. 'What impressed me particularly was the power with which not so much whole poems as particular combinations of words worked on my mind', Barfield writes in *Romanticism Comes of Age*. 'It seemed there was some magic in it; and a magic which not only gave me pleasure but also reacted on and expanded the meanings of the individual words concerned.'

This experience then feeds back, so that the extraordinary enhances what had been ordinary before. Barfield continues, describing how his new perception of the words in poems had an impact upon his perception of the world around him too:

> *The face of nature, the objects of art, the events of history and human intercourse betrayed significances hitherto unknown ... I found I knew (there was no other word for it) things about them which I had not known before.*

He was raised an agnostic, took no drugs, as far as I know, and had been sceptical of claims to a spiritual side of life. And yet he managed to keep focused on these novel experiences, rather than trying to explain how or what was occurring. They showed him a way out of what he calls 'the vacuum', an empty view of life.

Many, many other similar cases could be cited. William James catalogues dozens of examples, adding, 'We are alive or dead to the eternal inner message of the arts according as we have kept or lost this mystical susceptibility.'

Mystical experience is not just associated with the arts. Nature prompts it too. James includes the confession of Charles Kingsley, the Anglican clergyman and early champion of Charles Darwin.

> *When I walk the fields, I am oppressed now and then with an innate feeling that everything I see has a meaning, if I could but understand it. And this feeling of being surrounded with truths which I cannot grasp amounts to indescribable awe sometimes ...*

What appears to happen is that Kingsley gains a glimpse, as if in the corner of his mind's eye, of a dialogue and intelligence that he normally takes to be the nodding of heads of grass, the shifts of wind amongst the blades. Being surrounded by such ineffable truths prompts a deep sense of participation with the world. He is no longer outside or above it. The distinction between subject and object collapses. The world is now intersubjective. He is in it, so that its meaning is his meaning too. To be momentarily attuned awakens him to the reality of his own soul.

This, then, goes some way to answering our first question, what mystical experiences are like. The extraordinary breaks into the ordinary, and thereafter, the ordinary takes on a new sheen. Such experiences can be prompted by the arts, by nature, by the sacred, by drugs. So what of the second question: are ordinary experiences so different? I actually expect not much. What is different, though, is that we usually do not pay much attention to our ordinary experiences. It probably takes an extraordinary, religious-like experience to inject a sense of surprise. When that happens, we find that the ordinary is not so ordinary at all.

The world as it is lived

One philosophical movement of the twentieth century has tried to revivify the felt sense of everyday life, not via religious experiences, but by examining it in minute detail. The aim is to stay with the experience itself, rather than stepping back and objectifying it, as is the habit of modern science. The method is known as phenomenology, after the Greek for 'to show' or 'to appear'. It is the study of the givenness of the world, the world as it is lived, as it shows itself, as we feel it.

For example, the science of optics tells us that we see things because light reflects off the surface of objects, hits the retina in our eye and the resulting electrical impulses are processed in our brain. That is true, but it is an objective account of what happens. The phenomenology of sight is different. It is fascinated by the way that we can gaze out at the world. We can hold something in our sight, we can intimidate or welcome someone just with a look. Some force, invisible to optics, comes out of our eyes too. The philosopher Ludwig Wittgenstein caught it well when he noticed,

'The ear receives, the eye looks ... one can terrify with one's eyes not with one's ear or nose.'

What is even more surprising – though is, in fact, also an everyday experience – is the way that things in the world can grab hold of us too. This happens most obviously with other people. To have experienced love at first sight is to have had all your attention drawn suddenly towards one person, like a weathercock swinging abruptly with a change of wind. You are struck by Cupid's arrow, it is said, or assailed by your beloved's look; you can't take your eyes off them. More generally, people routinely get under our skin. We say that we can't get them out of our heads, or shake them off.

The same can happen with apparently inanimate objects too. Remember what it was like the last time you had the leisure to contemplate the indigo blue of the sky on a clear, bright day. The experience is not just of the scattering of light, as science explains, which occurs more with blue light, lending the sky at the zenith an almost purple intensity. For we humans, we sensors, something more is involved. It is as if the sky speaks to us – which is why 'blue-sky thinking' is a synonym for brainstorming: a thought arises that we did not expect; it is given to us from out of a clear blue sky.

The poets are alert to this active sensibility. It is perhaps what awoke in Barfield; indeed, Wordsworth once became troubled by a blue sky, as he reflects in his poem 'Tintern Abbey':

> ... And I have felt
> A presence that disturbs me with the joy
> Of elevated thoughts; a sense sublime
> Of something far more deeply interfused,
> Whose dwelling is the light of setting suns,
> And the round ocean and the living air,
> And the blue sky, and in the mind of man

It is striking that he links the blue sky and the mind of man, the object and subject, collapsing the divide. His perception is intersubjective.

Perception was explored in great depth by the phenomenologist Maurice Merleau-Ponty. He too describes the everyday experience of gazing at the blue sky. We do not study it, he thought, as the scientist might measure the elevation of the sun. We do not possess it, as if we have understood its blueness due to scattering. Rather, 'I abandon myself to it and plunge into this mystery, it "thinks itself within me", I am the sky itself as it is drawn together and unified, and as it begins to exist for itself; my consciousness is saturated with this limitless blue.'

Merleau-Ponty believes this is not a special experience. It is just what happens when we perceive. He goes on to describe how 'the outside' has ways of 'invading us'. In other words, it is not outside at all. It is linked in with us. It is just that we normally don't think much about it. So it takes a so-called mystical experience to draw us back to the wonder of the ordinary.

But this is what it is like to experience such mundane qualities as hardness and softness, light and dark, the desiccated and the damp. They are not registered by us in the way that a meter might specify their strength. We feel their impact; they might provoke us to flinch or smile, to exclaim fear or delight. 'I surrender a part of my body, even my whole body, to this particular manner of vibrating and filling space known as blue or red', Merleau-Ponty continues in *The Phenomenology of Perception*. Felt things express themselves to us; they speak to us. The experience may be so powerful that it can be like coitus, Merleau-Ponty muses, intercourse between oneself and the world. In perception, my body opens up to things, like a lover. Hence I experience my body as living, because the world lives with me.

Merleau-Ponty was also interested in the effects of drugs. He describes at some length a mescaline trip, during which proportions and perspectives shift and change:

A limb or other part of the body, the hand, mouth or tongue seems enormous, and the rest of the body is felt as a mere appendage to it … Sometimes motion is no longer seen, and people seem to be transported magically from one place to another.

What he realized is that such drugs do not cause completely novel experiences, delusions that come out of nowhere. Rather, they play on the normal processes of perception and, given the right conditions, alert us to their mystery. They resonate with the psychology of the individual too, of course, which explains why the ancient shamans put such store by preparation. For the experience to be discerned aright, it is not just enough to pop a pill. Mind and body must be brought into the best frame for the doors to open.

Reminders of reality

It seems that drugs undermine the valorization of objectivity, which has become so desirable in the scientific age, and brings many good things in its wake. So, the assumption that the impartial view is truest, and the surrendered view is weak-minded or absurd, needs to be challenged. Drugs are one way to do this. They will augment and distort, for sure. They artificially induce expanded states of consciousness. They are used, if you dare. But the experience is not automatically inauthentic. It might lead to the recovery of awareness.

The sadness is that it might require powerful drugs, often distributed and consumed in dangerous and uncontrolled environments, to gain a sense of the mystical in the ordinary. The modern world is not, on the whole, enamoured with the discipline and patience required to follow the older spiritual paths, or to contemplate the often difficult insights of the phenomenologists, for that matter. But if the prevalence of illegal drugs is any indicator, it seems that we long to see the world afresh again.

James thought that stimulants, intoxicants and the like are today commonly misused for precisely this reason.

The sway of alcohol over mankind is unquestionably due to its power to stimulate the mystical faculties of human nature, usually crushed to earth by the cold facts and dry criticisms of the sober hour. Sobriety diminishes, discriminates, and says no; drunkenness expands, unites, and says yes.

Similarly, an overly wary scientistic scepticism that mocks spiritual experience and lambasts mystical traditions can see nothing transcendent in the extraordinary everyday – and seeks to see nothing transcendent in the extraordinary everyday. It rejects the possibility, concurs James, that 'our normal waking consciousness, rational consciousness as we call it, is but one special type of consciousness, whilst all about it, parted from it by the filmiest of screens, there lie potential forms of consciousness entirely different'. Hence,

> *It is not just enough to pop a pill. Mind and body must be brought into the best frame for the doors to open.*

it is a kind of wilful blindness to argue that because entheogens or magnets around the brain effect altered states of consciousness, these experiences are empty and vain. Only a mind that has lost touch with the remarkable nature of perception could reach such a reductionist conclusion. The experiences can be reminders of reality rather than prompts to superstition.

Some scientists realize as much. 'Of course, far from invalidating religious experience [neuroscience] merely indicates what the underlying neural substrate might be', notes V.S. Ramachandran, the eminent neuroscientist. But the move from explaining in part to explaining away is an easy step to take. 'We may go through life without suspecting [different forms of consciousness]', reflects James. 'But apply the requisite stimulus, and at a touch they are there in all their completeness.' And that completeness matters. 'Looking back on my own experiences', he concludes, 'they all converge towards a kind of insight to which I cannot help ascribing some metaphysical significance.'

CAN YOU BE SPIRITUAL WITHOUT BEING RELIGIOUS?
Organized religion is clearly flawed, but spirituality struggles without it

A *man describes two or three occasions in his life when his perception of things seemed to shift radically. They were short, intense periods of transcendental feeling, almost visionary. The external world became 'enlarged and clarified to include many things, all of which I was able to see without losing sight of everything else', he writes. But what had he seen?*

The expansive sense was not the result of drugs or a recent traumatic event, like the death of a loved one. One occasion was on a beach, another on the London Underground, another on a bus that was winding its way from Charing Cross Road to Barnes. The setting was entirely ordinary. And yet they were moments when this world took on a different depth. He continues:

These visions of the real world were laced through with patterns and connections and correspondences. They were accompanied by a feeling of intense, calm excitement. I felt that I was seeing the truth, that all things were like this and that the universe was alive and conscious and full of urgent purpose.

The man who experienced these shifts of consciousness was the best-selling author Philip Pullman. He was writing in the *New Statesman* magazine. His confession struck me as particularly arresting, as Pullman is a self-identified atheist. He sees no sign of God in nature and is strongly committed to a materialist world view. Whilst fascinated by religion, he believes that the speculations of theology and the myths of traditions are inventive but fictional, ingenious but unlikely. As a result, he distances himself from interpreting such visions as religious – or spiritual, for that matter, a word he resists because he can't make much sense of it either. But why? What is it that has become so difficult about the word 'religious' that even when individuals have powerful experiences of the transcendent they resist naming them so? And what is lost in that resistance, which is another way of asking our question: can you be spiritual without being religious?

The struggle for authority

The word 'religious' has become so awkward that even regulars at churches and temples will insist that they are 'spiritual but not religious'. In Pullman's case, one element of his anti-religiosity is easy to spot, because it forms a key thread in his trilogy of brilliant stories, *His Dark Materials*. In them, the religious people are the bad people. They serve an entity called the Magisterium that mistakenly believes it is putting the world to right, though it destroys everything of value in the process, twisting and perverting what is innocent and true. It is a body, served by the equivalent of priests and prophets, that is determined to control by deliberately deploying lies.

The trilogy is a compelling indictment of centralized, hierarchical religion. Power is the problem, and it's a case that is easily made. Take Christianity. In Jesus's own lifetime, whilst he was still with them, the disciples quarrelled with one another about who might have greater authority. In a way, that is entirely to be expected. They were trying to respond to a tremendous experience, the unsettling life of this exceptional figure and the part they might play in furthering his message. It was too much for them, too insistent to be parked, as you might a brief moment of apparent transcendence on the bus

> *What is it that has become so difficult about the word 'religious' that even when individuals have powerful experiences of the transcendent they resist naming them so?*

or tube. It demanded radical change, a conversion of life, though how, in what way, to what end? And they were still human. Little wonder that the disciples squabbled about their roles.

Christians have a disastrous tendency to come to blows, witnessed to by the tragic fact that within two years of the emperor Constantine converting, and making Christianity the official religion, Christians started persecuting one another to the death. The fact is doubly cheerless because this happened easily within living memory of Christians themselves being bloodily persecuted by the anti-Christian emperor Diocletian.

So Pullman has a point. When Christianity became the religion of choice for the powerful, the struggle over meaning was compounded by the struggle for authority. The property and possessions that belonged to a now empire-wide institution were at stake. To tap that wealth meant you had to serve the institution, which, it hardly needs saying, is not necessarily the same thing as serving the inspiration left by the founder of Christianity, Jesus. The vitality of the spirit can readily be confused with the vitality of the organization, but whereas the former celebrates the virtues of faith, hope and love, the latter will reward abilities to do with management, loyalty and clout. After Constantine, theologians did not seek the spirit so much as patrol the borders of belief. By donning the old imperial purple, popes showed that heaven was a place on earth, and they were in charge.

> *When Christianity became the religion of choice for the powerful, the struggle over meaning was compounded by the struggle for authority.*

Further, and ramping up the risk of corruption again, priests were told that they were a tribe set apart. They were not like other men. They could cure souls. From that, it is a short step to the assumption that priests are more virtuous than others too.

This is a powerful illusion that obtains to this day. Churches routinely demand more exacting lifestyles from their clergy than they do from the laity, as if celibacy or poverty were ways of ensuring that clergy are morally superior. Bertrand Russell, who was keenly aware of the failures of religion, summarized the ensuing peril in his essay 'Religion and the Churches': 'Any average selection of mankind, set apart and told that it excels the rest in virtue, must tend to sink below the average.' Pullman's fictional Magisterium corresponds well with the actual magisterium. It makes even good people do bad things. It perhaps encourages vice more than virtue.

The problem is not confined to Christianity. The ancient Jewish people knew that division is a constant threat in organized religion too. Israel itself means 'one who strives with God'. The same tension can be seen in Islam and Buddhism, and no doubt any philosophical system that seeks institutionalization: atheistic movements go in for bickering, fighting and assassination too.

The conclusion is that religious organizations are more or less destined to become fight clubs. They have internal laws that try to contain the violence; they will talk of the need for unity and champion the virtue of compassion. But the violence is only abated, not stopped. Hence, many people opt for a policy of doing away with organized religion altogether. Better not only to be spiritual rather than religious, but to avoid being religious if you seek to be spiritual.

Knowledge is power

A second negative association that has become attached to the word 'religious' is specifically modern. It regards religion not only as all too human and flawed but as conservative and retrogressive, as a debilitating tie to the past. It is a prejudice that arises from the relatively recent notion of progress.

Progress as the organizing principle of social life and human learning emerges in the West at the time of the Renaissance. The works of ancient writers such as the politician Cicero, the historian Tacitus and the architect Vitruvius flooded back into Europe. Individuals from Petrarch to Machiavelli were enormously excited by them: Machiavelli describes returning home at the end of the day and discoursing with the ancients: 'Received amicably by them, I partake of such food as is mine only and for which I was born.'

Renaissance man cultivated himself, and as he did so, he simultaneously defined himself over and against his medieval forebears. The schoolmen of the Middle Ages, as they were known, were weighed down by sophistry, it was said. It was the Renaissance humanists who spread the rumour that scholastics spent days trying to calculate the number of angels that might dance on the head of a pin.

The new man, in contrast, was drawn by vibrant, personal ideals. The old schools had written in turgid Latin, whereas the new learning spoke in elegant Italian, English and French. They went so far as to invent a typeface for their texts: italic. The scholar who defined the historical study of the Renaissance, Jakob Burckhardt, summarized the shift in *The Civilization of the Renaissance in Italy*: 'In the Middle Ages ... man was conscious of himself only as a member of a race, people, party, family, or corporation ... In Italy this veil first melted into air ... man became a spiritual individual, and recognized himself as such.'

At the turn of the seventeenth century, one man turned this attitude into a programme that has subsequently shaped the world. He was Francis Bacon, a high-flyer in the English Elizabethan court. He described a way of systematizing Renaissance advances to ensure that knowledge grew steadily and cumulatively, 'to keep it from leaping and flying', as he wrote in *Novum Organum*.

Bacon was penning the philosophical basis of what we now call science, possibly the most successful creed the world has known. He believed that discovery and invention, experiment and enquiry were not just pursuits for the intellectually curious, but had the capacity to drive humanity forward, onwards and upwards. 'Knowledge itself is power', he wrote, echoing the book of

Proverbs. We can no longer be 'lookers on', passive contemplators of nature and her mysteries, but must commit to this mission, to progress. It is our destiny, he construes, and it will be ours so long as the learned cooperate and the sciences stay active.

Bacon was not anti-religious. Quite the opposite. 'A little philosophy inclineth man's mind to atheism, but depth in philosophy bringeth men's minds about to religion', he insisted in an essay, *On Atheism*. His conception of science had not narrowed to today's physics, chemistry and biology but included all the sure knowledge to which humanity aspires. There is a science of spirituality too. But his philosophy had the effect of taking knowledge from the hands of God and God's church, and placing it in the hands of well-educated men and women – a good thing, you might think, though if they could shrug off ecclesiastical authorities, they might become little less than gods themselves. There is a dignity in humankind that rests on this godlike freedom of discovery, wrote Bacon's Renaissance predecessor, Pico della Mirandola. Pico imagines God speaking directly to humanity, circumventing His old representatives on earth, the priests and prophets: 'Thou shalt have the power, out of thy soul's judgement, to be reborn into higher forms, which are divine.'

Medieval consciousness was transformed into Burckhardt's 'spiritual individual', and Renaissance individuals like Bacon recognized themselves as such. The long-term effect of Bacon's anthropocentric progressivism is that the accumulated wisdom of old religious traditions looked first less relevant, then an impediment to progress, and finally – to many – ridiculous. Hence, another reason that people today can conclude that religion stands in the way of genuine spiritual insight, and so call themselves spiritual but not religious.

You see this broad sweep played out in Philip Pullman's novels too. The children in his stories, with whom the reader sides, are lively, imaginative and questing. They are accompanied by what Pullman calls daemons – spiritual companions that delightfully change shape and form. These 'soulmates' are full of passion, an excitement that only subsides as the children become adults and their daemons become staid and steady.

Compare that liveliness with the heavy religious figure of the Authority, the One whom the Magisterium services. A godlike entity, he appears at the end of the trilogy, though he does not inspire fear and awe, as you might expect, but powerlessness and pity. He is pathetically borne on a bier and then dies, with a look of 'profound and exhausted relief', as Pullman describes it. The Authority is a religious, deathly force, the enemy of freedom and progress.

The perennial philosophy

Further factors have deepened the wariness of religion in recent years. There is the high profile afforded to fundamentalism (see *What is it Like to be a Fundamentalist?*). There is the spread of a form of individualism that is wary of joining organizations, including religious organizations: it runs with the assumption that joining means submitting and so relinquishing the freedoms of self-determination. And there is a relativism that concludes that if all traditions could be right, then no tradition can be right. Hence, if you visit the many summer festivals that take place in the country parks and stately homes of Britain, you will find an area designated 'The Spirit Zone', or something similar, offering experiences from introductory meditation to aura healing. But you will not find an area designated 'The Religion Zone'. Similarly, in bookshops, the shelving space set aside for books on mind, body and spirit far outstrips that dedicated to theology. All in all, the implication is that it is good to be spiritual, bad to be religious.

And who would disagree, bar the occasional bishop in purple who might discern his power fading in the turn towards such free thinking? Well, for all the flaws of organized religion, there are reasons to be sceptical of the apparently spiritually liberated.

One problem is an assumption that beneath the corrupted veneer of religion lies a pure spiritual essence. It is commonly called the perennial philosophy, and the implication is that the individual who is spiritual but not religious is seeking to find this timeless teaching. When describing his transcendent experiences, Pullman posits this possibility. He borrows from William James, observing that James 'ignores the theology and looks calmly at the psychological effects and consequences of belief, making human sympathy the key to his basic approach'. Pullman agrees that theology is regressive and the so-called golden rule – only doing to others as you would have them do to you – is the factor common to all religions worthy of the name. Human sympathy is the essence. You can ditch the rest.

Most religions do include the golden rule somewhere within their teaching, it is true. But I suspect that this process of extraction renders this rule, or any other presumed essence, more or less meaningless. The broader context is needed to give weight to the moral injunction and spiritual insight.

The philosopher Immanuel Kant recognized this difficulty. He called the golden rule 'trite', when considered in isolation. Could not immoral characters, like criminals, cite it in a plea to ease their punishment? Would you want to go to prison if you were in the position I'm in? they might implore. Kant reasoned that it cannot always be right to obey the golden rule, because if you always don't-do-to-others-as-you-wouldn't-have-them-do-to-you, then all kinds of other moral values are undermined, like the justice of sending a criminal to prison.

More generally, religious traditions can't all boil down to the principle of human sympathy, not least because human sympathy is such a transient sentiment. As work on empathy shows, it is relatively easy to muster good feeling when you are dealing with people who belong to your own group. But the connection that bonds you to your own kin is also likely to lead you to reject those who are from different groups, whom you are likely to perceive as a threat. It takes more than a vague ethical aspiration to overcome that.

Sympathetic love, Plato observes, is widely thought to be morally admirable. But it is easy to love your friends. So wouldn't the true moral hero be not the person who loves his friends, but the person who can love his enemies – those with whom he has little natural sympathy? This is more challenging than the golden rule.

Another problem with seeking a spiritual essence is that it leads to a shying away from searching out the meaning of spiritual experiences, being content to remain with the 'pure conscious events' as if they held meaning in themselves. Oceanic experiences count more than tricky philosophy. Much of this attitude stems from the work of Abraham Maslow, the psychologist of the 1960s. He devised a hierarchy of human needs, placing spiritual belonging at the top. At the time, he did much to humanize a discipline that was inclined to treat human beings as little more than rats with a remarkable ability to find their way out of mazes. But unfortunately, Maslow's hierarchy tends to nurture a fuzzy kind of spirituality. It resists discernment in favour of nebulous good feeling, and so empties religious experiences of the meaning that might be gained from them when they are situated in a religious tradition – a tradition that has the resources to interpret what might be being said about human nature, about reality, about God.

> *The most valuable spiritual insight lives on a knife-edge between pure intuition and careful discernment. You need both to keep your balance.*

This would be to treat religious experiences as just one part of what the philosopher Spinoza called 'the intellectual love of God', a phrase that is almost incomprehensible to today's spiritual searcher. What has 'love' got to do with 'intellectual'? the hippie-inclined might ask. However, this is an association that goes back at least to Plato, for whom 'mind' and 'spirit' were almost interchangeable. It's tough, because organized religion so clearly goes wrong, but those who seek the life of the spirit need to engage in the life of tradition too.

Denys Turner, the philosophical theologian, describes it well: 'Intellect is the place of light, for the light in which we see, and reason, and judge, and calculate, and predict, and explain ... that light is in us, but not of us.' The point is that the most valuable spiritual insight lives on a knife-edge between pure intuition and careful discernment. You need both to keep your balance. Someone who lives only by spiritual experiences and refuses the insights of the ages risks constructing a life that claims to be open to everything, but in reality is so baggy as to have little of tangible worth in response to the big questions of existence: who are we, what are we for, how is life made, what most truly is?

morality, creativity, spontaneity, problem solving, lack of prejudice, acceptance of facts — Self-actualization

self-esteem, confidence, achievement, respect of others, respect by others — Esteem

friendship, family, sexual intimacy — Love/belonging

security of body, employment, resources, morality, the family, health, property — Safety

breathing, food, water, sex, sleep, homeostasis, excretion — Physiological

MASLOW'S HIERARCHY

If these other questions concern you, then the religious part matters. Churches and their human traditions are a necessary evil. If it is hard to live with them, it is probably harder to live seriously without them. For whilst the history of religious organizations is pockmarked by misdeeds and transgressions, they are also the repository of a wisdom that any one life could not hope to sift and accumulate. Be conscious of their worst, but at their best, a commitment to a religion is an invitation to be part of a process of spiritual questing that, with its symbolism and fine music, its community and best thinkers, its genius and flaws, will engage you at every level of your being.

Philip Pullman's hesitancy about naming his religious experiences 'religious' is understandable. His wariness is a typically modern attitude born of an awareness of the failures of history and the hope of progress. But to stay with the protest is to risk staying your spiritual life. You can be spiritual without being religious, but you might not get very far.

HAVE YOU SEEN A MIRACLE?

The power of perception and the issue of divine intervention

*T*he *world miracle comes from the Latin* miraculum, *meaning something that is an object of wonder. 'To live at all is miracle enough': this marvellous observation was made by Mervyn Peake, author of the Gormenghast novels, and it is a common one throughout religious texts. 'The heavens declare the glory of God', wrote the author of the psalm. And yet today, people tend to mean something else by the word.*

Instead, they will say that a miracle is a divine intervention, a godly conjuring trick, a spiritual interference. Or as the philosopher David Hume defined it: 'a transgression of a law of nature by a particular volition of the deity, or the interposition of some invisible agent'. These kind of miracles don't elicit a 'Wow!' so much as a 'Yikes!'

Hume provides what some believe to be the definitive refutation of the possibility of miracles. The argument runs like this. If you take a miracle to be an exceptional intervention in the usual course of things, then it is only natural to ask for convincing evidence of that interruption. But that will be very hard to produce. After all, the definition of miracles, as exceptional interventions, is based on the assumption that everyday life is probably without miracles. So, given the obviously humdrum nature of the vast majority of our experiences, it is surely only reasonable to assume that they are all of the same routine status

— even those rare events that appear to be miraculous. The astonishing is almost certainly deceiving.

Did someone walk on water, or are those making the report mistaken? The latter is more likely by far. Was someone miraculously cured, or is not a much better hypothesis that the person went into remission or recovered by entirely natural, if rare, processes? That would be consistent with our usual tried and tested experience.

Hume continues, driving his argument home. Any evidence for what is claimed as an exception and a miracle, he writes in *Dialogues on Natural Religion*, would have to overturn the massive probability that the person making the claim is in error. That would, in itself, be a kind of miracle. So it is always going to be far more plausible to assume that the person is misguided than that the claimed miracle actually occurred. As Hume sums up, in his slightly convoluted way: 'No testimony is sufficient to establish a miracle, unless the testimony be of such a kind, that its falsehood would be more miraculous than the fact which it endeavours to establish.'

> *Given the obviously humdrum nature of the vast majority of our experiences, it is surely only reasonable to assume that they are all of the same routine status — even those rare events that appear to be miraculous.*

Miracles occur everywhere

There is no doubt that the search for miracles is often, in the lives of believers, akin to a search for divine intervention. Worse, the desire for such miracles can readily become a form of superstition. The bones of a saint or the power of a holy man's prayer are felt to be like spells. They perform a kind of magic that intrudes on the normal course of events by means of supernatural power. Why else would our medieval forebears have flocked to Rome to see the Sudario, the cloth allegedly used by Veronica to wipe the face of Jesus, when it was put on public display in 1300? 'It was the most remarkable thing that was ever seen, that during the whole year there were in Rome, besides the Roman people, 200,000 pilgrims, not counting those who were coming and going along the roads', recorded Giovanni Villani, a Florentine chronicler. Why else would Frederick the Wise have amassed a collection of relics that by 1520 had grown to over 19,000 in number?

Well not, in fact, for the magic. Or for a miracle as a kind of intervention. Or at least, not officially.

Monotheists such as Christians, Muslims and Jews have been persistently warned against theurgy, as it is also called – rituals performed to provoke God into unusual action. Theurgy comes from the Greek for 'God' and 'work' and can be rendered 'working the divine'. It was condemned, along with magic, because it implies that God can be manipulated at the behest of human beings. Pull the right string and God must respond, like a puppet. That can't be right, because it would mean that God is subject to human wilfulness and wishes, an inversion of the real relationship between the human and the divine.

There is, rather, something else going on with these relics and sacred places, and their attendant stories of the miraculous. It has nothing to do with the Humean interventionist understanding of miracles and everything to do with the miracle as something that evokes wonder. This alternative argument goes like this.

For monotheists, God is everywhere and so God's power is everywhere too. It is as active in the breath you take as it is in the blessing offered by a saint. However, inhaling and exhaling are humdrum, so the believer can easily overlook the wonder of life in a breath, whereas receiving the blessing of saint is an exceptional experience, and so stands out. It might feel like one of the high points of your life. And yet, in truth, all it does is make visible what is often obscure or overlooked by distracted mortals – like the marvel we call breathing. Holy things, then, should be desirable to the believer only because they make the everyday power of the divine clearly manifest. That is their gift. A miracle properly understood shows, in fact, that it is not exceptional.

You can see how this might work by the explanation provided alongside a large collection of miraculous stories collated by Gregory of Tours in the sixth century. It amounts to eight books in total, and the tales they contain are often extravagant. Phantoms drag off frightened peasants and are only tamed by God. Gregory himself seems to have suffered from a succession of oral complaints. Once, a fishbone stuck for days in his throat. Another time his tongue swelled up, causing him to stutter. The dust from the tomb of a saint cured both. So was the dust a kind of sacred potion? No.

> *Holy things should be desirable to the believer only because they make the everyday power of the divine clearly manifest. A miracle properly understood shows that it is not exceptional.*

It was the intense experience of holiness, prompted by Gregory's proximity to holy objects, that catalysed the change. 'Often ill people acquire cures by means of these tokens', he writes. 'But what do I dare to say about them, since faith believes that everything that the sacred body touched is holy?' And if the token is holy, then everything is holy, since everything is touched by God the creator. Hence, it is Gregory's argument that miracles occur everywhere too. The reason he records so many miracles is not that miracles are rare, but that they happen all the time. It is just that people only notice them when they seem out of the ordinary, and so miss the miracle of their usual well-being.

This is to challenge the common assumption that miracles are exceptional. It was an argument made fully by the theologian Thomas Aquinas. Again, his starting point is that God is already deeply active in everything. What we call natural activities – those that obey the laws of nature – are as much a part of God's doing as those that seem to fall outside of the laws of nature or are not covered by the laws of nature. It makes no difference to God, as He is the sustainer of all things.

It follows that God cannot be said to intervene, perhaps to cause a so-called miracle, because He is never not at work anyway.

71

If someone assumes that God intervened in one moment, and that they have witnessed a miracle, that implies that they think He hasn't intervened in another moment. That is simply wrong, Aquinas asserts. All of life – all of the cosmos – is directly and continuously attributable to God, the creator. The baker who makes 5,000 loaves is as involved with divine providence as Jesus was when he distributed loaves to the 5,000 in the gospels. Both are marvellous, properly perceived.

That is not to say that what happened when Jesus distributed the loaves is not hard to spell out, from this distance. Given for the sake of argument that we are supposed to accept the story in a literal way, it is clearly not the kind of thing that happens every day. Aquinas also argues that as God is the reason why there are natural laws, so it must be perfectly within God's capabilities to do things not covered by natural laws. But though unusual, the feeding of the 5,000 is no more miraculous than the baker's involvement in the wonderful process that combines flour and yeast, salt and water to make deliciously fragrant fresh bread.

There is, therefore, nothing exceptional about the unusual events sometimes called miracles, so far as faith is concerned. The whole of existence is itself already miraculous. If some particular event seems miraculous to a believer, the correct response is not to focus on the extraordinary but to be reminded of the 'ordinary' gift of life itself. 'There is nothing that God hath established in a constant course of nature', preached John Donne, 'and which therefore is done every day, but would seem a Miracle, and exercise our admiration, if it were done but once.'

Shifts in perception

There is another way of looking at this older understanding of the miraculousness of every moment. If life itself is amazing, then the question stops being about how to bring about a miracle, and becomes how to perceive the miraculous that is already happening all around.

It was this question that occupied religious thinkers of the Renaissance. The humanist philosopher Marsilio Ficino, for example, borrowed from the tradition of the followers of Plato. There was an old Greek saying he liked: 'Nourish the cock, but do not sacrifice him, since he is sacred to the sun and moon.' It is the ancient equivalent of the Christian worry about theurgy. Don't kill a chicken believing its death will bless you or curse an enemy, it warns. The chicken's life is sacred too. Instead of attempting to work on God, work on yourself. We are often so confused, continues Ficino, that we are scarcely able to discern the wonderful capacities with which life normally empowers us, to say nothing of the tremendousness of life itself. So still your confusion, he implores. Calm your spirit. Then you will see the power of the divine – of life – all around and flowing through you.

Ficino was particularly struck by the promptings of dreams. On one occasion, he dreamt that he would be healed of an illness. The dream seemed to promise him an early return to good health, which, upon waking, proved to be true. What is striking is how he interpreted the dream. It did not cause the change, he believed. Rather, it offered him a tranquil state in which he could detect the early signs of the welcome restoration to health. If only he could be so alert to life in the everyday.

We can develop this understanding of miracles a stage further by focusing on the shift in perception they might provoke – the change that suddenly sees the wonder of a grain of sand, or 'heaven in a wild flower', to quote William Blake.

With an eye for the miraculous, a new world comes into view. It is like what happens should a blind person regain their sight or someone who is deaf their hearing. The cure is not what overwhelms them. It is seeing and hearing for the first time. Such a new life would be radically different from the one before. They would continue their lives in a different world, a world remade anew – with sight, with sound.

The philosopher Ludwig Wittgenstein made this observation in his *Tractatus*: 'The world of the happy man is different from that of the unhappy man.' His point is that the way to understand happiness and unhappiness is not to think that the two people live in the same world and just have different moods. They actually live in entirely different worlds, the difference springing from their different perceptions – one happy, the other sad. Similarly, when someone close to you dies, the sadness weighs on every moment. The cosmos greys. Conversely, when you fall in love, the joy colours each breath.

So too with a miracle. It enables the individual to break with the old and enter a new existence. Thereafter, the world never looks quite the same again. This is why a conversion can be regarded as a miracle. It is a complete reorientation of life. 'The man's hard heart may soften and break into religious feelings', as William James describes it. Or it is why Christians regard the resurrection as a miracle: it is not because something exceptional has happened – Christians believe that all will be resurrected at the last day: then, there will be overwhelming evidence. Rather, the miracle of Christ's resurrection reveals that tremendous hope.

Modern psychology offers another angle on this view, in the explanations it gives for cures that might be regarded as miraculous. The British psychotherapist Donald Winnicott tells one story that seemed like a divine intervention, though he has a better account of what happened. It concerns a baby girl of about a year old. She had been brought to Winnicott, who was also a paediatrician, because she was having fits. The fits had started following a period of illness in which she didn't eat well, became irritable and then apparently lost interest in life. It seemed she might die.

Winnicott saw the child for just 20 minutes each day, and after about a month she was completely cured. It seemed like a miracle to the mother, who must have feared the worst. However, Winnicott explained things differently.

The fits were not caused by a neurological disease but were rather a result of a psychoneurosis. The illness had led the child to become withdrawn. He suspected that the fits started when the child's loneliness turned in on itself. His cure was to pay careful attention to the youngster as a person, not treat her as a medical case. That drew her out of herself again and the fits stopped.

More generally, this is to recognize that human beings are psychosomatic creatures. We are many-aspect wholes. Sometimes attending to the soul is what a person needs, and when that has an impact upon physical health, the effect can seem miraculous, particularly to the materially minded.

Better, though, to see that the 'miracle' reveals a deeper truth about ourselves, one readily forgotten because treating people as machines to be fixed, as much modern medicine does, is successful in so many cases. But not in all. Then, the attention of a therapist can have a healing effect. An empathic word can be as powerful as a drug. One person speaks to another, and provides

Sometimes attending to the soul is what a person needs, and when that has an impact upon physical health, the effect can seem miraculous.

the sick or injured party with a sense of significance and meaning once more. Instead of leaving the psyche out, it is attended to. The personal and spiritual needs of the individual are satisfied. Physical changes may well result too.

Viewed in this way, then, what miracles show is that we are more complex and subtle than the imagination can sometimes allow. The cure catalysed by a therapist – or a priest or a visit to a holy shrine – is only a reminder of our psychosomatic nature and how amazing that is.

Every pebble is an exception

There are other reasons why the understanding of miracles as aberrations of the laws of nature is so unsatisfactory. What I am thinking of now is that the idea of miracles as divine interventions assumes something about the laws of nature that may well, in fact, not be so. The assumption can be put like this: the natural world is causally closed. In other words, there is a continuous unbroken causal web that links every event with every other event. It is as if, given the precise coordinates and exact momentum of every particle at time 't', it would be possible accurately to predict just what the cosmos would look like at time 't+1'.

But modern physics suggests that that is not so. There appears to be a fundamental indeterminacy running through things. For example, a nuclear physicist can tell you how long it will take a lump of uranium to lose its radioactivity, but he or she can tell you nothing about which atom of uranium will discharge its radioactivity next.

This is to say that the laws of nature are probabilistic. Think of it this way. Imagine having a jar full of pebbles. You can determine the average weight of the pebbles by weighing the lot and dividing by the number of pebbles in the jar. Say the average is 50 grams. If you then reached into the jar expecting to pull out a pebble weighing 50 grams, however, you would almost certainly be disappointed. In fact, to pull out a pebble with that weight would be something of a miracle.

So while no laws of nature are broken, every pebble is an exception. In such a probabilistic world as ours, it makes very little sense to talk of miracles as unusual events, as every event is unusual, simply by virtue of being itself.

The situation is worse than that, thought David Hume. Not only is the universe not causally closed. It is far from clear what it would mean to link a cause with an effect in the first place. He asked whether anyone has ever observed a cause in action, and concluded that this would be impossible to do. You may think you have witnessed a cause when you see the white snooker ball hit a red one, causing the red one to drop into the pocket. That, though, would be wrong. All you have seen is the white ball move, then the red one. You infer, quite naturally, that the impact of the white ball on the red one will lead to the pocket. It's a sensible inference, but only an inference.

Interestingly, the medieval Islamic philosopher al-Ghazali presented a similar argument in the eleventh century. He too reasoned that there is a logical gap between causes and events. However, the same observation led him to a very different conclusion from Hume. For al-Ghazali, it was proof positive that God must be the real cause of every event. Only that could account for the fact that the world keeps going.

In such a probabilistic world as ours, it makes very little sense to talk of miracles as unusual events, as every event is unusual, simply by virtue of being itself.

Such thoughts are somewhat esoteric. Not many of al-Ghazali's Muslim peers agreed, as indeed not many contemporary philosophers followed Hume's radical causal scepticism. However, the basic point remains.

It is easy to assume that by a miracle people mean a divine intervention. However, if you follow this definition then you will be beholden to search for evidence to prove it – evidence that will always be questionable. Worse, theologically speaking, the belief that God has intervened to cause the miracle carries the implication that He is not involved at other times.

Theologians such as Aquinas argue that this is false. Every moment of every day and night rests on the sustaining power of the divine. Existence itself is the miracle. What this adds up to is that experiences that people call miraculous are really only a particular case of what is generally true. Life is wonderful, amazing. All in all, as George Bernard Shaw suggested, a miracle is not about proof and exceptions. It is merely 'an event that creates faith'.

WHAT IS THE LITERAL MEANING OF SCRIPTURE?

On reading between the lines and making the text work

It seems extraordinary to me that individuals who claim to read the Bible do not know that there is more than one creation story in the book of Genesis. You can get that just by reading the first couple of chapters. And yet people who claim to know the Bible will argue that it tells you, quite straightforwardly, that the world was created in six days. Until the nineteenth century, however, hardly anyone took literal accounts of biblical creation seriously. It was ridiculed by Talmudic scholars, church fathers and Martin Luther, the Reformer.

The truth is that Christians and Jews have always read the Bible in enormously inventive ways. How could it be otherwise? Truth resides with God alone, so whilst God certainly reveals Himself, that revelation must of necessity always be oblique, enlightening while holding on to mystery. Human language always falls short. If the believer thinks that they've understood God, they are not worshipping Yahweh but what the Hebrew Bible spends more verses condemning than anything else: an idol.

Augustine's 'real truth'
In the Christian tradition, a master of faithful Bible reading is Augustine, the towering theologian and bishop of the early church. He is a good person to reference because he wrote a

multi-volume book entitled *The Literal Meaning of Genesis*. What is striking is that his deployment of the word 'literal' meant almost exactly the opposite of what it describes today.

For Augustine, the 'literal meaning' is the 'real truth', not the 'plain sense'. He writes, 'In all the sacred books, we should consider the eternal truths that are taught, the facts that are narrated, the future events that are predicted, and the precepts or counsels that are given.' He asks whether biblical narratives should be taken as a 'faithful record of what happened' or whether they have a figurative sense. His answer is perhaps surprising: 'No Christian will dare say that the narrative must not be taken in a figurative sense.' In other words, he agrees with St Paul, who in the First Letter to the Corinthians, referring to the story of Moses, writes not that those things actually happened, but rather, 'Now all these things happened unto them for examples: and they are written for our admonition.' The 'literal' meaning of the Bible is that which matters now. It is understood in the impact upon the lives of believers. Scripture is a living word. Allegory is life-giving, and literalism, as meant today, is life-denying.

> *Truth resides with God alone, so whilst God certainly reveals himself, that revelation must of necessity always be oblique, enlightening while holding on to mystery.*

This means that discovering the real truth of scripture is a hard task. On one level, it requires us to penetrate the text, meditate upon it, bring to bear all the resources at our disposal, and wait for meaning to emerge. At another level, reading the Bible places huge demands upon us, for we must undergo a personal preparation, even purification, to understand it clearly. In his most famous book, the *Confessions*, Augustine describes the interaction between text, believer and God, praying that God will allow him enough time to discover the text's inner meanings, and that he himself might be adequate to receiving what it has to say:

Open the door to them when I knock on it. You had a purpose in causing the Scripture to contain so many pages dark with obscure meaning. This dense wood shelters deer who have taken refuge in it, restoring their strength, pacing its lanes and grazing there, resting and ruminating.

As a result, Augustine's reflections on the meaning of Genesis are fascinating. For one thing, he does not believe that the six days of creation contained in the first story of the genesis of the cosmos actually means six days. He insists that it cannot. The Bible cannot contradict reason, and reason tells him, via the work of the ancient Greek astronomers, that the world is round. This means that daytime on one side of the Earth is night-time on the other. So when Genesis describes the evening and morning of the first six days, that cannot mean straightforwardly that there was a first day, and so on, for one country's daytime is another country's night. 'If I said such a thing, I dread being a laughing stock among those who are scientifically informed', he reflects. It is for this reason that the scholar Garry Wills prefers to translate from the 'literal meaning' the title of Augustine's book as 'first meanings', stressing that the effort of reading is in discerning what the symbols deployed in the text are trying to tell us. (My quotes from the *Confessions* are from the excellent translation by Wills.)

> *Scripture is a living word. Allegory is life-giving, and literalism, as meant today, is life-denying.*

Consider Augustine's reflections on 'In the beginning God made the heaven and the earth.' God's making, he begins, cannot be like human making, because, unlike God, when we make something, we are always already part of a long tradition of making that thing. Consider a book. An author will have read many books, toyed with the different forms and styles others have used, considered how they resonate with his or her own character and aims, and above all will be utilizing language – that complex of words and syntax that has evolved over aeons.

God's making is not like that at all. He begins at the origin of all things. So when God 'says' let there be light, nothing is heard, because there is no medium in which the sound waves might propagate. There is no first moment of sound, an arc of loud divine expression, and then a dying away, echoing the meaning of the great fiat. This is because in the beginning, God creates time too, from all eternity.

This is a mystery, though one which reflection on scripture and experience can illuminate. It prompts Augustine to ask about the nature of time. For we humans, he says, time is intimately bound up with memory. He derives a schema in which time is experienced as a reaching-out from the present into the future and the past.

Imagine you are about to sing a song. (Augustine imagines he is about to recite a psalm.) In your mind's ear, as it were, you can hear the song in its entirety. You can imaginatively sense what you are about to sing over the next few minutes. As you prepare to sing, your mind reaches into this future.

When you actually start to sing, your mind's ear is turned in the opposite direction, towards the past, and the times you have sung the song before. As you breathe and open your mouth, your singing reaches back into the past, to bring the song into the present.

The mystery of time and memory, then, is that it allows us to reach into the past and project into the future, the present being the passing moment 'through which what was future is being shuttled into what is past'.

But then Augustine adds a further twist. Time must be measurable. We say that a period of time endures, for a second, for a minute, for an hour, for a day. But the present doesn't endure, it being the passing moment between the future and the past. Neither can the past be said to endure, because it no longer exists. Nor the future, because it does not yet exist. It seems,

Augustine concludes, that our experience of time actually contains an intimation of timelessness. The present, past and future have a quality of timelessness because none of them, in fact, endure, for all that we casually say they do. We experience the present, the past and the future by the action of our memory, reaching into the future, reaching back into the past. It is as if we hover in the present on an edge between time and eternity.

Augustine's reflections on a simple sentence of Genesis have carried him a long way! There is nothing straightforward about reading the Bible at all. Though for his reward, he feels he is being given an intimation of the eternity of God, whilst also slipping and sliding around the bizarre, mortal experience of time. 'I cannot put time together in my mind, my very thoughts are shredded, my soul inwardly unstrung', he cries to God, 'til I flow together in you, purified, to melt into the fires of your love.' This is what it is like to read scripture.

One faith, different modes

Perhaps surprisingly again, Augustine had little interest in historical questions. If someone had proposed going to search for Noah's Ark on Mount Ararat, say, he would have laughed. If someone had devoted time and energy to writing a book on whether Jesus's tomb was empty on the third day, he would have sighed. He much preferred to ponder the allegorical and prophetic meaning of the Bible for the Christians of his day. Even quite straightforward passages of scripture will have many layers of significance.

Further, he is comfortable with various interpretations of scripture being possible: that is bound to be so, because the value of the Bible, its truth, is found in an interpretation that is applied to a particular set of circumstances. What matters is that the application is faithful. There is 'one faith, different modes'. Diversity is a blessing, and when human readers delude themselves that their reading is right and fixed, they have made themselves into gods; they have placed themselves above scripture. A good reader must be honest, open and prepared to put up with the toil of mental struggle. To such readers, the Bible will become all the more valuable.

The process Augustine describes could not be more different from many of the modern debates about the Bible, the protracted and vociferous rows about the historicity of the six days of creation, the literal truth of the resurrection of Jesus, and other historical questions. And yet today it is common to find mainstream theologians insisting that unless all these 'events' are literally true, the Christian faith is in vain. Christianity is not a moral philosophy, it is declared. It is an historical event, inaugurating the new creation that Christians are in the business of realizing.

To my mind, such approaches demonstrate so much of what is wrong with the contemporary religious imagination. It shapes the way people read the Bible with a spirit very much of the modern age: to be true, something must be empirically verifiable, historically determinable and irresistibly right. Allegory and meaning, symbol and archetype are for spiritual types. Such arty sorts read the Bible as if it were Shakespeare or Plato, a kind of life-enhancing entertainment. No: the truth of the gospel must force itself upon you, as robust as a physical law that can smash an atom. But it leads to all sorts of absurdities.

Why are there four gospels, not one, which differ in so many details? Or why did Jesus believe that the world was about to end, and yet it is still here, 2,000 years on? If you go down the literalist line, you spend a lifetime trying to justify the historical inconsistencies and hiatuses.

Paradoxically, if you make the Bible a book of evidence, you wring it of its real power, the subtle quality that has kept it living for generations. If faith stands or falls on its provability, it's likely to fall. And you miss the main point. Of course faith must relate to what can be ascertained of historical events and facts. But to be faith, it must be more expansive than textual tests or empirical seizure allow. If you adopt Augustine's strategy, you can freely, imaginatively, truthfully interpret the text to ensure it stays alive. Scripture must be more than a commonplace book, more than an historical record, more than a moral guide, more than wise counsel on the human condition. It's why many traditions insist that their holy texts are sung, not read. That is the first way a Muslim is supposed to hear the Qur'an.

Ironically, it can be those who read the Bible from outside the faith who develop a keen sense of its vitality. They never thought it was literal, in the narrow sense, and so are free to approach it with an open spirit. One such person is Melvyn Bragg, author of *The Book of Books: The Radical Impact of the King James Bible 1611–2011*. 'I am still unable to cross the River of Jordan which would lead me to the crucial belief in a godly eternity', he has written. Looking across the Jordan, though, seems a good vantage. He is able to express the power of the Good Book with a rare passion.

> *Scripture must be more than a commonplace book, more than historical record, more than a moral guide, more than wise counsel on the human condition.*

The Bible can be a dastardly tome, Bragg acknowledges. Christian history is full of times when the Bible 'has been the best man at . . . a bloody wedding'. The Hebrew Bible relates such bloody encounters on its own pages. But that is only to say that ideology can bend the text its way. That is the risk of interpretation, though one that must be run if the words are not to die on the page.

And Bragg sees the influence of the Word in many historical turns for the good too. The abolition of slavery is one. For almost every civilization, for much of human history, slavery was accepted as a necessary institution. Different times and places might prove better or worse for the slaves. But slavery itself seemed inevitable.

It took the Bible to shift that apparent necessity. No book of ethics managed it. No political text either. It was William Wilberforce, who read the King James version every day and had its cadences and rhythms, as well as its message and meaning, running through his veins, who persuaded the British Parliament to sign the crucial abolition act.

On the other side of the Atlantic, amongst the African slaves of America, the Bible was the tome of freedom too. Those without any freedom, let alone freedom of speech, could feel free when they opened the pages describing the liberation of the Hebrews from Egypt, which insisted that even death is no barrier to the love of God. 'Let my people go', it declares. This is deep culture, Bragg explains. It both describes the predicament of slavery, giving it voice, and taps a wellspring for music and a message that would gather pace over the decades. Now, America has a black president. There is a result for the 'literal' meaning of the Bible.

It's an impressive history. But if Augustine urges biblical literalists to consider the text again, what of secular readers today? How might they read it?

A living text
It perhaps helps to consider a religiously neutral text, though one that I find you can read time and time again and discover something new with every iteration: Plato's *Symposium*.

The *Symposium* consists of a series of speeches about love, made by a group of Athenian men attending a dinner party. What they say is troubling, inspiring, beautiful, dark, insightful, easy and difficult in equal measure. And it can be read in one of three ways.

The first is a rational way, as if it is a kind of puzzle. Each speech can be assessed in turn, and the one that offers the most coherent, useful or novel account of the subject concerned might be taken as Plato's unique contribution, and hence the *Symposium*'s real message. Only that would not make it a text to return to, as once you'd cracked it, you could move on. Similarly, scripture is not a puzzle.

It can be read in an ethical way, as if it is an exploration of the different ways in which we humans try to love, hope to love, and fail to love. Each speech portrays different accounts of this everyday and yet problematic urge. We seek to honour love as the highest good, though we dishonour it in our actions too. We seek to make commitments to those whom we love, though relationships break up. It's the *Symposium* as an account of the wisdom and virtues we need to cultivate if we are to love not wildly but well. Only once more that does not do it full justice, as something more than that is going on in it. Similarly, there is more to the Bible.

Third, it can be read in a spiritual way – by which I mean it is a text that grapples with a phenomenon that it does not ultimately understand. That is surely Plato's genius, and to this extent he is like the authors of the Bible. He conveys this sense that we'll never have love sussed, by creating a text that can be read in innumerable ways, its patterns shifting like a kaleidoscope. It deploys myth as well as reason, darkness as well as light. Are the speeches independent and/or more subtly linked? Is the goal of love the beatific vision described at the end, or is that route sheer folly, as other characters imply? Is love part of the comedy of life, or one long human tragedy – though a tragedy that can ennoble our experience and make us the envy of the gods? Is it neither, or both?

It's impossible finally to decide. There is no one reading of the *Symposium* that is definitive. Love, like life, is both of us and beyond us. And this is why the *Symposium* is a living text, and worthy of comparison with the Bible. (Augustine believed that Plato was seeking after God too, in his own way, and so could have accepted this analysis.)

Ultimately, the Bible is not rational or even ethical; it is not a distillation of wisdom or a consolatory read. Rather it's a living text. This is why it has inspired art and further literature, architecture and generations of human beings. It forces us to read between its lines to glimpse something of the mystery of life, and thereby to want to make something of love, of freedom, of experience, of God – the most tremendous energies of life that it tries to convey.

IF YOU'RE NOT RELIGIOUS, IS NOTHING SACRED?

Art, children, life itself. A lot is still surprisingly sacrosanct

*S*ome people fear that as belief in God becomes a private matter, so sacred values decline. Others welcome the development, arguing that notions of holiness hinder humankind. But is the sacred any less potent a force today than it was in the past?

In 1911 the *Mona Lisa* was stolen from the Louvre in Paris. The thief was Vincenzo Peruggia, an otherwise unobtrusive carpenter who worked in the gallery. He kept Leonardo's portrait in a box in his apartment for the next two years before he was discovered trying to take it to Italy, which he believed to be its proper home.

What is extraordinary about the theft is that more people went to gaze at the empty space the year after the elusive smile disappeared than had looked at the picture the year before. People woke up to what had been lost. Its absence asserted its status. The image was then mass-produced, with facsimiles popping up in private living rooms and on hotel walls. People wanted a share in the magic. It is now the most famous painting in the world.

If any work of art can be called sacred, it is the *Mona Lisa*. It is a one-off original and carries the hallmark of genius. Who would disagree that the world would be a worse place if it did not exist or disappeared from view? Hanging once more in the Louvre, it is afforded a reverence akin to the Holy of Holies in an ancient temple. This is the real thing; Leonardo's own hand brushed it. It has intrinsic value. We are encouraged to approach

THE *MONA LISA* (*C.* 1503–6) BY LEONARDO DA VINCI IS AN EXAMPLE OF THE SECULAR SACRED.

the image with humility, almost an attitude of worship – so long as we can elbow our way through the straining crowd.

Describing the present and absent quality of that famous smile, in an article on the image for the magazine *Prospect*, the philosopher Roger Scruton put it this way:

> *It conveys the highest gentleness to which a human being can attain – a gentleness almost divine. Mona Lisa looks into the heart of the viewer in something like the way Christos Pantokrator looks into the soul of the one who worships him. This image fascinates us because it steps out of our world . . .*

He continues, noting that an icon like the *Mona Lisa* can be desecrated, as Marcel Duchamp did when he adorned the face with a beard and moustache. But if it can be desecrated, that is only because it has first been consecrated, by human feelings.

A taste of the transcendent

Great works of art provide examples of how the concept of the sacred appears remarkably persistent in a secular world. Originally, the word had a clear and specific meaning. A person, object or place was sacred if it was consecrated to a god, for a purpose that was distinctive from the humdrum or profane. The saint was venerated. The statue was hallowed. The temple was holy. Various penalties would be imposed if the sacrosanct was violated, penalties that are known as sanctions – another word that displays its origins in the notion of the sacred, the root being the Latin *sacer* or holy.

> *Great works of art provide examples of how the concept of the sacred appears remarkably persistent in a secular world.*

However, because of these strong religious connections, a long and rumbling row can be heard in the contemporary world about whether anything should be called sacred any more. Clearly, few would today regard the Parthenon as sacred because it once housed the holy statue of Athena – though many people sense that churches, synagogues, mosques and temples still in use carry a quality of sacredness. They are happy to remove their hats or, conversely, cover their heads when entering, as a mark of respect. But then such buildings serve explicitly religious purposes.

What is surprising is that sacredness is ascribed to things that are not religious. And so a question arises: in a secular age, can life be called sacred, or can virtues like trust, or relationships like marriage? Debunkers of sacredness say not. They insist that to resort to its rhetoric displays a weakness for redundant superstitions and a refusal to engage in rational arguments about why, when and how we should value things. They would prefer to hold the debate about abortion, say, or euthanasia without the encumbrance of life being declared sacred, which they take to mean off-limits – though I suspect that what it really means is not that life cannot be ended, but rather that when a life *is* ended, it is important to recognize it as a real loss.

Then there are protagonists who wish to hold on to the category. They worry that when you can't deploy the term, all manner of supremely precious things are lost sight of, perhaps even the value of life itself. 'People will do and say anything, and . . . nothing is sacred', observed the artist J.G. Yeats, brother of the Irish poet. The idea of the sacred still carries a power, they believe, regardless of whether someone sees themselves as religious. A photo of their beloved is sacred to them. The life of their child will surely be so.

And many objects too, if great art like the *Mona Lisa* is any witness. Such originals capture our imagination in a special way, as the critic Walter Benjamin explained in *The Work of Art and Mechanical Reproduction*. A work like the *Mona Lisa* has a 'presence in time and space, [a] unique existence at the place where it happens to be'. Standing in front of it, we can sense a direct and timeless link with the creator, a knowledge of the piece as embedded in a meaningful tradition, an aura felt by virtue of the viewer's proximity to such an extraordinary, almost other-worldly object. The analysis might add that it takes a degree of effort to visit the place where the sacred object is kept, much as a medieval pilgrim had to journey to reach the building that held a relic. The original also speaks of what we call authenticity, another component of the modern concept of the sacred.

The power of the sacred goes so far as to make art an ersatz religion. It offers a kind of salvation, Benjamin continues, and takes on a 'redemptory function': when listening to or standing before great art we can find momentary release from the demands of the everyday, much as our forebears presumably found consolation in honouring a deity or saint. Art transforms the mundane as the temple used to do. It offers a taste of the transcendent.

And yet, Benjamin was ambivalent about treating art as sacred. He observed that modern art in the form of photographs and film can be endlessly reproduced by mechanical means. This means that it makes little sense to talk of an original, and even less to talk of the aura of the work – a change that has a plus side. Modern art is liberated from the cult-like rituals associated with the appreciation of the Old Masters or the statues of ancient Greece.

There are other ways of attempting to refute the staying power of the sacred that otherwise secular people seem incapable of not ascribing to great art. One atheistic voice might argue that even the best copies of a work of art will fudge the small details that make a massive aesthetic difference. That's why we want to see the original, not because it is sacred. Another might make the argument that the original appeals because it provokes greater imaginative engagement with the work, though that is really a sentimental fantasy. However, both these attempted deconstructions of the notion of art's sacred value are instrumental: you need the original to see the image at its best. The whole point of the sacred, though, is that it moves beyond the instrumental, and into the realm of the intrinsic, the set apart, the holy. It matters in itself. It should not be violated. So long as you accept that some things in life have such worth, it seems you are forced to accept that the concept of the sacred carries meaning.

The 'universe story'

If anything, the secular age is characterized by a renewed interest in what can be called sacred. It is becoming increasingly common, for example, quite self-consciously to create sacred stories concerning no less an object than the universe itself.

The new myth derives from the latest science. The standard model in physics, based upon the Big Bang, tells us that out of this primordial miracle emerged first energy, then particles, then atoms, then simple molecules, then dust, then nebulae, then stars, then heavier atoms, then complex molecules, then planets and galaxies, then stable environments hospitable to life, then life, then complex life, then conscious life, then self-conscious life – then us.

> *The universe seems to have embarked upon a process that led inexorably to creatures with the ability to look out across the cosmos whence they came, and understand and contemplate it.*

Each stage in this evolution produces a new phenomenon that couldn't be predicted from what went before. More remarkably still, the universe seems to have embarked upon a process that led inexorably to creatures with the ability to look out across the cosmos whence they came, and understand and contemplate it.

The reason advocates of this so-called 'universe story' want to celebrate and propagate it is that they believe the modern world is losing touch with the wonder of things. We are in a predominantly mechanical, materialistic phase that has led to a desacralizing of the cosmos. That may yet have disastrous ecological consequences, given the predictions of climate science, though the worst might be abated by recovering 'the ancient ideas of sacred groves or holy springs', as the cosmologist Brian Swimme and the ecologist Mary Tucker hope in their book *Journey of the Universe*. They continue:

> *The deep truth about matter, which neither Descartes nor Newton realized, is that, over the course of four billion years, molten rocks transformed themselves into monarch butterflies, blue herons, and the exalted music of Mozart. Ignorant of this stupendous process, we fell into the fantasy that our role here was to reengineer inert matter.*

The science of the twenty-first century is correcting this profanity. The story of the universe is being recognized as one of 'creative emergence'. Echoing the intonation of the book of Ecclesiastes, Swimme and Tucker stress, 'There was a time for bringing forth hydrogen atoms. There was a time for bringing forth the galaxies. There was a time when Earth became ignited with life.' These are deep processes, revealing the 'sacred depths of nature', as another scientist, the biologist Ursula Goodenough, has described it.

The universe story forms itself into a social programme and religious creed. Here's how another couple, the physicist Joel Primack and the philosopher Nancy Abrams, formulate it in *The New Universe and the Human Future*, a book based upon their contribution to the prestigious Terry Lecture series.

> *We have to admit the disastrous course of business as usual; invest in scientific research, including in the social sciences, to find all possible openings; agree to a great extent on what can be done; negotiate in good faith as to who will do what; and stick with the overall plan through thick and thin, despite inevitable short-term crises.*

This, they continue, must become a global article of faith and honour 'just as serious and indeed sacred as upholding the cosmos was to the ancient Egyptians.' And, as if that were not enough, they go on to invoke cosmic sanctions should human beings continue to violate the sacred universe.

> *Earth is negotiating with us right now and waiting, not so patiently, for a good-faith reply. If humans don't make it, the universe has plenty of time and space to try and evolve intelligence again, but humanity will be sloughed off as if we had never been.*

Some will find themselves strongly disliking such sacred myth-making, even laughing at it, for all that it draws on science. In quieter moments they may be prepared to share the ecological alarm that lies behind the desire to tell of the 'sacred depths of nature', and to admit that in times of environmental crisis, invoking the sacred may be required to galvanize enough action to stem disaster. Only they would prefer to do so without deploying the religious language. But can that be done?

The philosopher Ronald Dworkin made a serious attempt in his book *Life's Dominion*. He agrees that 'we want to look at one of Rembrandt's self-portraits because it is wonderful, not that it is wonderful because we want to look at it'. More generally, art and life can carry this intrinsic value because it is '*independent* of what people happen to enjoy or want or need or what is good for them'. Hence, 'something is sacred or inviolable when its deliberate destruction would dishonor what ought to be honoured'. Honouring the universe is partly what tellers of the universe story call for.

The analysis allows Dworkin to make some useful distinctions. There are things that are regarded as sacred but have no intrinsic value. A national flag would be one example. Conversely, knowledge has intrinsic value, though it is not regarded as sacred – setting to one side the sacred knowledge that theologians have argued is given to believers as divine revelation.

However, Dworkin is to my mind less successful in developing a secular language of the sacred. He argues that it would be a 'cosmic shame' if, say, species of animals and plants that exist now ceased to be because of human actions. But the word 'shame' makes the destruction sound like a necessary mistake rather than a sacrilege. The language of honour too, whilst carrying moral weight, falls into a lesser category than that of the sacred. Honour has to do with pride, dignity, respect, admiration. In the case of art, we might say that honour belongs with the artist, but not with their masterpieces. These we afford a different status, that of sacredness.

The sacredness of the individual

Maybe there is another way to address our question. We began by noting that there are some who want to argue that nothing is sacred if you are not religious, not because nothing is of immense value, but because the concept of sacredness has become superfluous, possibly offensive. However, that did not seem to work. Many people value things as sacred – from great art to our own universe. That happens regardless of whether they think of themselves as religious. The conclusion would be that, like it or not, the sacred is a necessary category when engaging with the things that we rate as of weighty, non-negotiable significance. Nothing else will quite do.

So perhaps we shouldn't worry. The religious person can take the persistence of the sacred as indicative of the lasting value of the religious imagination, the sense human beings have that some things serve a greater purpose. The non-believer can accept the sacred as having performative value: like curses such as 'Hell!' or 'Hocus-pocus!', the language of the sacred originates in a bygone age, but can carry stress and substance today. Either way, the fear that 'nothing is sacred' is an unnecessary worry. It is quite clear that human beings cannot but ascribe sacredness to certain things. The real question is what.

> *Like it or not, the sacred is a necessary category when engaging with the things that we rate as of weighty, non-negotiable significance.*

This line has been developed by the sociologist of religion Gordon Lynch. Looking back to the work of the sociologist Emile Durkheim, he believes that every society needs concepts of the sacred to sustain its cohesion. The only difference is that whereas in ancient societies the sacred focused on the gods, in modern societies it focuses on human individuals. In *The Division of Labour*, Durkheim wrote: 'Whoever makes an attempt on a man's life, on a man's liberty, on a man's honour inspires us with a feeling of horror in every way analogous to that which the believer experiences when he sees his idol profaned.'

This is not, in fact, a rational concept, for all that philosophers might defend the language of human rights using reason. The sacredness of the individual is based upon a stronger emotional conviction, which is to say that it has to do with how we experience ourselves and how we relate to others. Nothing less than horror overcomes us when we see another's life taken, another's dignity profaned – and if someone didn't share that horror, we would spontaneously sense that they were inhuman.

The sacred has always carried the notion that it should be treated in ways that are different to everything else, and this is what we instinctively feel about the human individual today. If morality means anything now, it means guarding and cherishing what is of human worth – and nothing will be of human worth if human beings aren't treated as such. It should matter very much when these values are desecrated.

This does not mean that everyone will agree on what is sacred. The psychologist Scott Atran makes this clear in his book *Talking to the Enemy: Violent Extremism, Sacred Values and What it Means to be Human*. His extensive experience of talking with perpetrators of various forms of terrorist violence has led him to conclude that sacred values lie at the heart of these twenty-first-century conflicts. Further, until they are recognized as such, they are conflicts that will escalate and perpetuate, not be won or lessened. Importantly, the sacredness of certain values is held by individuals on both sides. It is the clash of these values that causes so much distress.

> *To be human is to hold some things as sacred. Not to do so would make us less than human.*

Across the world, people believe that devotion to sacred or cultural values that incorporate moral belief – such as the welfare of their family and country or commitment to religion, honour, and justice – is, or ought to be, absolute and inviolable.

What this means in practice is that trying to pay off Palestinians, say, for land that they regard as sacred and their own will not work. That is only to insult them. More optimistically, though, research has shown that 'Palestinian hard-liners were more willing to consider recognizing the right of Israel to exist, if the Israelis apologized for suffering caused to Palestinian civilians in the 1948 war.' Such an apology would recognize the fundamental sacred issues at stake, and with that, the more humdrum negotiations about land might commence.

Raising the subject of terrorist conflict and the Middle East might lead not so much to the conclusion that there is nothing that is sacred in the modern world, but that there is too much that is held sacred. However, that would not be right. To be human is to hold some things as sacred. Not to do so would make us less than human.

CAN AN AGNOSTIC PRAY?

What prayer is, what prayer is not, and meditation

I'd like to propose a straightforward response to this question: I suspect it is only an agnostic who can pray. What I mean is this.

First, it can't be the case that only believers can pray. It might be assumed that this is so, on the grounds that only the believer knows who they are praying to. But I think this actually gets prayer the wrong way around. The most heartfelt prayers are often spontaneous. They are cries for help or shouts of thanks. Whether or not anyone is there to hear them is immaterial. In fact, if you were absolutely convinced that there was someone listening to you, you might not cry or shout out at all. You might reason that your divine hearer knows what you need or feel before you do yourself.

This is to say that prayer has directionality. It originates in the minds and mouths of men and women. It can be done by agnostics. It is likely to be done by agnostics for the very reason that they don't know, for sure. And further, there is something agnostic about all prayer, from agnostics and believers alike.

Turning to God

Prayer is common to all religious traditions, though it takes an endless variety of forms. Buddhists are best known in the West for meditating, while in the temples of Thailand and Cambodia, Buddhist prayer extends to making offerings to images of bodhisattvas and prostrating on pilgrimages and around stupas. Priests are sought for blessings. Hands are raised in the air.

One of the most impressive forms of prayer is the collective prayer of Islam, a requirement for Muslims, known as *salat*. It takes the form of deep coordinated bows and repetitions of symbolic words in the sacred language of the Qur'an, and is offered in the direction of Mecca. I witnessed the power of this prayer particularly vividly once when I was travelling on the edge of the Sahara desert. Our driver was devout and so we stopped at the appointed times, the vehicle pulling up in the middle of a dusty nowhere. I got out and turned around, aimlessly scanning the horizon. The rocks and dunes seemed to offer no distinctive feature of any kind. And yet he immediately knew the direction in which he was headed. He orientated himself by the sun and joined in prayerful worship with his otherwise invisible brethren.

The physicality of the act was vital. Turning the body is a step towards turning the mind and heart too. It is a gradual process; the fact that the *salat* is performed five times a day demonstrates Islam's recognition that an orientation towards God only comes in time, with practice. The faithful will know in which direction to turn, though spiritually they may remain disorientated. He or she seeks God and so seeking, prays. Only those who don't know God must pray. To this degree, they share the predicament of the agnostic. They have more confidence that the activity is worthwhile, but who God is and what He wants from them is probably little clearer.

Body and soul

It seems a pretty safe observation that people pray because life is full of doubts. They pray for mercy, they pray that they might achieve their best, they pray for healing, they pray for the dead. All such prayer comes from a place of concern. Prayer is the activity of the uncertain though hopeful, the distressed though loving. 'Fervently do we pray', declared Abraham Lincoln in his inaugural address of 1865, towards the end of the American Civil War, 'that this mighty scourge of war may speedily pass away.' He didn't know that the war would be spent in a few weeks. So he added, 'Yet, if God wills that it continue . . .' And that lack of knowledge about what the future holds is why he prayed.

But is there more to prayer? Is there any sense in which it can be said to work beyond sheer human expression? Prayer and similar activities have been investigated by science. The results are fascinating, because they reflect quite closely what the religious traditions tend to teach about prayer.

Some types of prayer are shown to have a positive benefit. Take meditation. It is proven to impact on various human aspects, from controlling depressive swings to increasing longevity of. It is for this reason that in Britain you can have lessons in practising mindfulness funded by the National Health Service. What is taught is a kind of essence of meditation, extracted from its Buddhist context, known as MCBT or mindfulness cognitive behaviour therapy. The research makes sense, as what mindfulness aims to achieve is an alteration in a person's attitudes towards their own thoughts so that they are able to train themselves out of the downward spirals of negativity and stress characteristic of mental ill-health, and avoid being perpetually caught up in them.

It appears highly likely that related practices would have similar benefits. *Salat,* a habit of sitting silently when the day is otherwise crowded with distractions, might do much for someone's sleep patterns or levels of anxiety. Being treated by a doctor with the time to offer human care, rather than only the time to diagnose a medical fix-it, would presumably aid healing too. The psychologist Carl Jung took seriously the fact that we are psychosomatic creatures, and so must attend to the well-being of our souls as well as our bodies. It came as no surprise to him when, from his earliest days as a psychiatrist, he observed that 'a suitable explanation or a comforting word to the patient can have something like a healing effect'. What such a word provides is a sense of meaning, interpretation and context. 'The doctor's words, to be sure, are "only" vibrations in the air, yet their special quality is due to a particular psychic state in the doctor', Jung explains. That 'particular psychic state' is nothing more mysterious than treating the patient as a person.

> *Prayer is the activity of the uncertain though hopeful, the distressed though loving.*

This is to be 'prayerful' in an older sense, of demonstrating honesty and sincerity; of being open. What meditation and prayerful attention have in common, at base, is that they are attempts to be open to the wellsprings and sources of life. It is for this reason that in meditation you are trained to pay attention to your breathing. Breathing is not merely a convenient motion upon which to fix, as if the ticking of a clock would do as well. It is not just a mechanical action, any more than the heart is just a mechanical device. To breathe is to live, and so breath carries symbolic value.

Similarly, meditation teachers encourage individuals to walk mindfully. The aim is now to pay attention to the soles of your feet. That generates a sense of slow rhythm, which is helpful, but also a sense of rootedness. Your feet stand where you stand. So the implicit question in the practice is: where do you stand – physically and spiritually?

In a more overtly theological guise, prayer could be said to be paying attention to the dependency of all things on God. It is to recognize that human existence is sustained by the divine; that the wonder of life is not merely the lucky chance of a billion evolutionary permutations, but that running through all that evolutionary activity is life struggling to realize itself more fully. Prayer, it might be said, aims to complete that process by reaching back or up to the source of life. Hence it comes most naturally to people in the moments when they most feel alive – out of elation or fear. Prayer is an expression of what it is to be alive. (Another side thought is that the first prayer in the Bible, in the book of Genesis, is Adam's exchange with God. Doubly interesting is that this prayer comes when Adam is hiding from God, having eaten the apple given to him by Eve. The story might be taken as implying that prayer is humankind's attempt to find a way back to life, back to God.)

Petitionary prayer

There is another kind of prayer. In fact, it could be the kind people most usually mean when they talk about praying, and is referred to as petitionary or intercessory prayer. Its guiding understanding is subtly different from the understandings of prayer considered so far. The activity now is not about meeting the frightening fullness of life, or at least not on the face of it. It has the aim of bending the ear of God in order that a specific need might be met in a way that the individual deems it should be. It's the kind of prayer a person might offer for a lottery win. Or a parking space at the supermarket.

There is something obviously ridiculous in this kind of heavenward ejaculation. It assumes a number of things: that life's worth stands or falls on convenience at the supermarket; that there is a divine power shifting the balls as they fall from the lottery wheel, a power that might be persuaded to tilt in your favour.

> *Prayer could be said to be paying attention to the dependency of all things on God.*

Above all, the individual who offers such prayers risks usurping the place of God, or fate, as if they could determine what should come to pass. They do not share the agnostic spirit; they act as if they know precisely what should come next. It is an instrumental, magical, almost exploitative attitude of prayer. And strikingly, it seems not to work.

Research published by the John Templeton Foundation in 2006 subjected this kind of prayer to randomized controlled trials. It could find no benefit to individuals recovering from heart surgery who were being unwittingly prayed for by others whom the patients did not know. O God, keep down the arrhythmia. O Lord, hasten the healing of wounds. This is prayer treated like a pill, as if it can be blind-tested. Except that a pill is a chemical intervention; its active ingredients, purified and well studied, are valued because they have specific effects. Prayer is more like love. It is typically unclear what results it will have. Whatever else it might be, prayer is not an aspirin. Little wonder the research found a negative result.

That noted, it simultaneously seems clear that people are bound to offer such petitionary prayers. Someone may feel embarrassed admitting that they sincerely pray to win the lottery, less so that they cross themselves when they run on to the football pitch, and certainly not that they pray for individuals whom they love and who are sick.

But there is a difference here. This is prayer that is human and personal. Praying for a friend who is ill, and hoping they will become well, is an expression of concern in the midst of uncertainty. It is agnostic on outcome, though wholehearted in intent, in the way that a treatment never could or should be. Further, someone who was absolutely confident that their friend would recover would be little motivated to pray for them. They might help by picking up the prescription, but would otherwise wait for the happy phone call.

So the personal prayer is a kind of petitionary prayer that is meaningful, and it is meaningful in another sense too, one picked up by the Dominican theologian Herbert McCabe. He agrees that petitionary prayer need not be about manipulating God, a belief that throws up all manner of objections of the kind that delight sceptics – from why God should show favour to one person and not another, to how He can possibly satisfy the full range of contradictory prayers that reach Him from across the human population. God's mind is not changed by prayer, any more than is the direction of fall of the lottery ball. Instead, in such prayers McCabe argues that God is 'doing something in me, raising me into the divine life or intensifying the divine life in me'. Prayer does not change God's will. Prayer moulds the individual's will to the typically unknown, unclear will of God. Again, this is the activity of those who don't know God, who share the agnostic spirit.

Prayer is more like love. It is typically unclear what results it will have.

Imagine praying for a fine day, McCabe suggests. What is going on? The prayer should not be conceived of as a spell against rain, so that when dark clouds mount in the sky, the individual curses God and themselves because they did not pack an umbrella. Rather, if a saint were to say such a prayer, it would be a preparation for an appreciation of the blessing of a fine day. McCabe continues: 'It means that I can truly describe the fine day not just as a fine day but as an answer to my prayer, in other words as a revelation to me of God's love, a sudden privileged glimpse of the generosity of God.'

In reality, it seems unlikely that a saint would pray for a fine day. He or she may once have done so, though now that they are a saint, they will have learnt to give thanks for all days, come rain or shine. Everything speaks to them of the glory of God. That is part of what it is to be a saint, to see life in this way.

> *Prayer does not change God's will. Prayer moulds the individual's will to the typically unknown, unclear will of God.*

But only because they prayed, for prayer would, as it were, make saints of us all. This is a slightly different point, the idea that by paying attention to what you pray for – praying prayerfully – you might be changed. To put it bluntly, and following the thought of another Dominican theologian, Victor White: people generally pray for the wrong things.

Prayer as self-discovery

White argued that people pray for the wrong things because they pray for what they feel they ought to, from fine days to pure feelings. In truth, though, and if they knew themselves well, they may not really want these things at all. They may pray for a fine day for the family outing because they secretly know that a fine day will ease the tension of being confined for long hours in the car sheltering from the rain. The true prayer, then, would be not to avoid the rain, but to avoid an ugly, painful exchange of words.

Or people might pray for pure feelings because they are afraid of the dark thoughts that spontaneously well up in them.

This is prayer as a form of papering over the spiritual cracks. The right prayer, the one they perhaps should say, is the prayer of the psalms. Not infrequently, the psalmist prayed that his enemies might be massacred and that evil people be cursed. Psalm 55 describes the disquiet of heart that arises when you are betrayed by your friends. 'We took sweet counsel together', the psalmist recalls, though now 'a horrible dread has overwhelmed me.' 'His speech was softer than butter, though war was in his heart; his words were smoother than oil, yet are they naked swords.' So what does the psalmist ask for? Forgiveness? Compassion? None of that. 'Let death come suddenly upon them; let them go down alive to the Pit.' This is what he really wanted. This is what he prayed for.

As it turned out, the psalmist's prayers were not, for the most part, answered. The story of the Israelites is a story of being destroyed by enemies at least as much as vanquishing them. But a substantial part of the value of the psalms lies in their honesty, in their extremes of feeling. The psalmist is not afraid to come into the presence of God just as he is. He does not try to hide his dark shadows, or don a false face. He prays passionately, troublingly, honestly.

This is to understand prayer as a form of self-exploration for those who can admit they don't know themselves as well as they ought. It is prayer as a vehicle for self-discovery because we are not transparent to ourselves. 'If we are honest enough to admit to our shabby infantile desires then the grace of God will grown in us, it will slowly be revealed to us, precisely in the course of our prayer, that there are more important things that we truly do want', adds McCabe.

Such prayer starts to look quite like mindfulness meditation. It too is a practice that encourages the individual not to control their thoughts on the basis that some are better than others. Instead, it allows all and any thoughts to rise and fall. They are regarded non-judgementally. This has at least two effects. First, it means that the thoughts don't become any bigger than they need to be: a thought that someone deems foul or embarrassing, and that they consequently try to suppress, will almost inevitably loom larger in their mind and have far greater purchase on them than it might do were it just observed or perhaps gently mocked.

Second, it means that the internal life of the individual becomes clearer to them. They get to know themselves better, if they can bear it.

That said, there is a difference between prayer and meditation. Meditation makes the assumption that the examination of the life of the mind is an isolated, solitary pursuit. People may meditate collectively, of course. There is disciplinary support in that. But at the end of the day, the individual is responsible for the extent to which they might change themselves.

Prayer assumes that someone else is involved in the process: the presence called God. God's involvement is not the same as when prayers are taken to be petitions. Instead, the assumption in Christian meditation is that human wills might be changed by prayer. Thomas Aquinas summed it up when he noted:

We do not have to present our prayers to God in order to disclose to him our needs and desires, but in order to make ourselves realize that we need to have recourse to his help in these matters . . . By praying we offer God reverence, inasmuch as we subject ourselves to him and profess, by praying, that we need him as the author of all that is good for us.

We pray, Aquinas continues, for much the same reason as we walk: to reach our destination. Alternatively, we pray for much the same reason as we eat: to be fed. Both activities change us too. To move to a different place is, to a degree, to become a different person.

The point of prayer

It is sometimes reported that meditation is a painful process. It is hard to sit still, and when you do still yourself, all manner of unwanted thoughts come to mind – like those that the psalmist wrote down. Theistic prayer adds another source of discomfort too.

The individual comes to realize that they are not self-sufficient, that they cannot save themselves. However, in time, they may come to realize further that there is a divine presence beneath and through all things who does will them well, and who might change their will towards that which is well too. This might be an endpoint for the prayer of the agnostic, or at least a new beginning.

Prayer is likened to breathing. You can skip more prayers than you can breaths, and hold off from praying for much longer than you can hold off from breathing, but the analogy implies that prayer is an activity that sustains the soul, much as breath sustains biological life. It may be performed absent-mindedly. It may become troubled or laboured. Few breaths are as satisfying as a lungful of Alpine air; so too prayers. But great people of prayer observe that praying must be done, as with breathing.

> *Prayer is more like love. It is typically unclear what results it will have.*

Seeing the point of praying, observed McCabe, is not the same as seeing the point of eating lychees. Pop a lychee in your mouth and you immediately taste the sweetness. Prayer is more like seeing the point of a work of art. You may well not understand it upon first glance. It may also be ruined by being hung in the wrong place, or with you in front of it in the wrong frame of mind. Only gradually, with patience, care and discipline, does the point of it emerge. But there is one thing that is absolutely required. You must look at it, spend time with it, sit with it. So also, it is said, with prayer.

IS RELIGION INHERENTLY VIOLENT?

Crusades, the evolutionary benefits of deities, and sacrifice

*M*arch, 1146. *A monk dressed in white robes stands on the hillside outside Vezelay in Burgundy, France. Through the trees it is possible to glimpse the abbey above him, one of the most beautiful buildings in Christendom. People have gathered from across Europe to hear him. His name is Bernard of Clairvaux, and he has been commissioned by the Pope to launch the Second Crusade.*

The Pope had picked his preacher well. This zealous man was a Cistercian, a relatively new order of monks with a passion for reform, and Bernard was their reformer-in-chief. They objected to the excesses of medieval monasticism, whose great and wealthy monasteries blurred the boundaries between powers secular and divine. Cistercians founded their houses away from the sinful taint of towns and cities, though their search for suitable backwoods reveals the extent to which their righteousness could lead them. Tales quickly emerged of the order destroying villages in order to free up the land. This spirit of ruthlessness in the name of God served Bernard well as he stood on the hillside and stirred the crowd to liberate Jerusalem, cleansing themselves and the holy city as they marched and waged war.

The spot from which Bernard spoke is marked today by a large rock topped by a simple cross. It is a modest monument for an event that still grips the imagination almost a millennium later. The medieval Crusades symbolize an association that has become fixed in many people's minds, a link between fanatical

> *It seems obvious to many that religion is an inherently violent phenomenon, from which it follows that the world might be a better place without it.*

religiosity and spectacular violence. It has been deepened by subsequent history, particularly the aftermath of the Reformation, when the so-called wars of religion killed millions in Europe.

The Enlightenment was partly a response to this bloodshed. No more should spiritual passions govern the soul. Instead, reason should rule. More recently, the rise of political Islamism has rekindled the imaginative connection. Be it bombers killing themselves in the name of Allah, or worldwide riots precipitated by cultural affronts to religious sensibilities, it seems obvious to many that religion is an inherently violent phenomenon, from which it follows that the world might be a better place without it. But is this association right?

Identifying with violence

Religious practices have long been associated with a certain kind of violence, namely sacrifice. The philosopher Charles Taylor explains that gods have always demanded that their human subjects kill in order to feed, placate or curry favour. In *A Secular Age*, he shows how this sacrificial theme persists in spiritualized forms of religion too. Now, the individual is encouraged psychologically to tame parts of himself in order to be cleansed and made whole. The pious will sacrifice sexual intimacy and become celibate, or they will periodically abstain from food.

There seems to be a human need underpinning this perennial motif, which Taylor articulates this way. The world is a violent place. Suffering is an ever-present danger. In death, it sentences individuals to a terrible, incomprehensible fate. One way of forcing meaning on to suffering, thereby making it more bearable, is to believe that suffering, renamed sacrifice, is integral to the divine economy. The gods destine our lives to be shot with pain, but it is for our own and the greater good, for all that we will never fully understand the meaning of the connection.

It is a short step from here to identifying with violence; in fact the identification can be seen every day. Ask yourself why people perform symbolically violent gestures, like punching the air or uttering an expletive, when they feel they've tempted or escaped the cruel vicissitudes of fate? It might be called the 'warrior response'. A warrior has to face down the possibility of his own death in order to fight well. It is said that the Spartans went to war assuming that they were dead already. This means that we confront the terrible fears that threats to life arouse in us by claiming that destruction for our own. A punch in the air or voluntary offering of your life to a higher cause allows you to regain a sense of control. 'What was terrifying before is now exciting, exhilarating; we're on a high', Taylor continues. 'It gives a sense to our lives. This is what it means to transcend.'

The religiously minded will go an extra step and make that transcendence explicit by personifying destruction in the form of particular gods. In Indian religion there is the figure of Kali-Shiva, 'she who destroys'. In Western religions there is Satan, 'the opposer'. And as if to demonstrate the universal nature of the theme, even rational atheists will, on occasion, do the same.

Sigmund Freud recalls the time his eldest daughter was gravely ill and he thought she would die. When he heard she had made a great improvement, quite spontaneously he threw one of his slippers at the wall. As it happened, the shoe hit one of his antiquities and it smashed. That further incident led him to reflect on why he had thrown the slipper in the first place. It seemed an odd gesture. What was the link between hurling an item of footwear and the recovery of his daughter? In *The Psychopathology of Everyday Life*, he concludes that it was a kind of sacrificial act, 'rather as if I had made a vow to sacrifice something or other as a thank-offering if she recovered her health!'

The logic of sacrifice

If this analysis is right, human beings might be said to have two religiously toned responses to the inherent violence of life. It can either be submitted to, as when making a sacrificial offering to a higher power. Or it can be claimed as one's own, by performing acts of violence oneself. The two responses can also be combined, as the philosopher René Girard has conjectured. He argues that sacred massacres, literal or metaphorical, provide a double satisfaction. First, the massacre is felt to be symbolically cleansing by being offered to a higher cause or a god. Second, the individuals performing the sacrifice simultaneously become violent themselves, as if they were holy warriors.

> *Religion is, in part, an expression of violence, but not the cause.*

This particular logic of violence, based on sacrifice, suggests that it is a product of a possibly universal feature of humankind. In this narrow sense of having a capacity to feel the power of sacrificial acts, it might be said that everyone is religious, with a lower-case 'r'. After all, to be human is to suffer. It is not religious belief that makes us violent. Rather it is violence that turns us to the intense motifs of sacrifice that are particularly fully expressed in religions. Religion is, in part, an expression of violence, but not the cause. If religion did not exist, human beings would be compelled to invent something similar.

Atheists may well resist this universalism. Such critics of religion come back with another twist in the grim tale. They argue that there is a difference because only religion can make us believe that it is justifiable to sacrifice human lives; because only religion can make us believe that human lives are subordinate to the higher value of a sacred cause. As is sometimes observed, it takes religious belief to make good people do bad things.

The philosopher Slavoj Žižek has written about this dynamic in his book *Violence*. 'It is the very belief in a higher divine goal which allows us to instrumentalize individuals, while atheism admits no such goal and thus refuses all forms of sacred sacrificing.' He continues that the reason why religious violence appears to be on the increase in the modern world is that people today find violent acts far more difficult to perform than our forebears, for whom violence was more present and visible.

Further, the modern person is encouraged to view life as a process of enjoyment and self-realization, unlike the ancient person, who accepted the omnipresence of suffering and did not so clearly distinguish the value of their own life from the collective. 'The large majority of people are spontaneously "moral": killing another human being is deeply traumatic for them', Žižek speculates. 'So, in order to make them do it, a larger "sacred" cause is needed, which makes petty individual concerns about killing seem trivial. Religion or ethnic belonging fit this role perfectly.'

Whether atheism is capable of decoupling individuals from the expressive power of sacrificial violence looks questionable, however. Take Stalin. Žižek argues that Stalinism, though inspired by the ideology of the atheist Karl Marx, was nonetheless religious in nature because it acted on the basis that anyone could be sacrificed in the name of material and technological progress. Hence, the Stalinist terror was in fact religious, because it was driven by service to a higher cause.

However, this seems to me to be playing with words, and showing precisely the opposite: namely that even atheists governed by atheistic creeds can instrumentalize individuals and default to forms of sacred sacrificing. The Russian dictator's biographer, Simon Sebag Montefiore, strikes a better balance. In *Stalin: The Court of the Red Tsar*, he shows that Stalin was more than capable of holding two contradictory positions at once. 'This atheist owed everything to priests and saw the world in terms of sin and repentance, yet he was a "convinced Marxist fanatic from his youth".'

It is also important not to forget the broader context of anthropogenic violence, of which explicitly religious violence is just one manifestation. The three-volume *Encyclopedia of Wars,* authored by Charles Phillips and Alan Axelrod, examines nearly 1,800 violent conflicts throughout history. It concludes that only 123 of them were religious. That's less than 10 per cent. Ridding the world of religion, were that possible or desirable, would have only a marginal impact upon humanity's capacity for violence.

A sense of the sacred

A deeper understanding of why atheism, in practice, offers no guarantees against the logic of sacrifice can be gleaned by turning again to the work of Scott Atran (see also *If You're Not Religious is Nothing Sacred?*). He charts research across a variety of terrorists who have committed or ordered gross acts of violence. The fact of the matter, Atran writes in his book *Talking to the Enemy*, is that some are religious, in the sense of self-identifying with religious traditions, and some are not. Before 2001, the secular and nationalist Tamil Tigers in Sri Lanka were top of the list of suicide attackers. In the Middle East, Lebanon used to be the place most at risk of suicidal violence, and again secular nationalism was the majority motivation. Atran continues:

> *There isn't much precedent in Islamic tradition for suicide terrorism. Modern suicide terrorism became a political force with the atheist anarchist movement that began at the end of the nineteenth century, which resembles the jihadi movement in many other ways.*

A sacred value has been insulted. Violence will likely follow.

What all people have in common, he continues, are sacred values, by which is meant principles and ideals for which we would die. It might be your child, it might be your country. It might be for the freedom of your fellows, it might be for the purification of your soul.

Atran has an evolutionary explanation for this prevalence. He believes it follows from the fact that human beings live in complex societies; or to be precise, a sense of the sacred is what enables us to live in complex societies. In terms of evolution, the great problem with living in such large groups is that it means you have to live and cooperate with individuals who are not your own genetic kin. It comes naturally to all animals to live with those to whom they are related, because that serves the preservation and proliferation of the common gene pool. It also seems natural to many animals to kill those of the same species with whom they do not share their genes.

'Fictive kinship' – living as if related – is the device by which human beings manage to overcome these limitations and stay together. And nothing serves this fiction better than a shared belief in a moral deity. If you feel beholden to, say, a creator god or a protector god, then it means you will be able to sublimate your own genetic interests to those of your group, who worship and serve the deity. Atran goes so far as to argue that the ideal of a universal brotherhood of all humankind depends directly on the development of monotheism, which is the doctrine of a deity upon whom all depend. With monotheism, there is no one outside of the group, at the highest level. If all serve the same God, then everyone has the potential to recognize that they are one.

But there is a downside. Deities are moral; that is, they make demands in return for their succour. Originating with a god, those demands are felt as sacred values. That means our ancestors, before monotheism, were always alert to who was in the group, who was outside of the group, who was threatening what was felt to be most dear to them – land, or beliefs, or comrades. Moreover, such keenness of attention is invigorating. It speaks of who the clan or tribe is. It fires moral passions, never more so than when violent conflict is involved.

This is our evolutionary legacy, and whilst not all people believe in gods any more, all people are left with the capacity to hold sacred values and to be thrilled by conflicts about which they believe themselves to be on the right side. 'If it bleeds, it leads', as the news editor instructs. None of this is rational. Generally speaking, people engage in violent actions because they feel they have to. They must defend the innocent against a dictator. They must fight the infidel who threatens their sanctuary.

That sacred values have such a hold over us is demonstrated by a quick thought experiment. Imagine someone asked whether you would hand over your child for a million dollars. You would be shocked and declare no. So they ask you whether you would hand over your child for two million dollars. Now you are not only shocked but annoyed, and say no once again. They come

back a third time and offer three million. You are now offended
and quite probably become aggressive. A sacred value has been
insulted. Violence will likely follow.

Leading by example

Such evolutionary stories are just one way of underlining the
apparently universal truth. Everyone has something for which
they would die, for which they would make the ultimate sacrifice.
The philosopher might add that it is not until you know what
you would die for that you also know what you would live for.
If you happen to be a religious person too, then your religious
tradition will supply copious resources to convert this gut instinct
into mythological, ritual and doctrinal expression.

It is for this reason that, in the past, violence was often
dressed with divine sanction – because the whole of life was
experienced through the social imagery of religious traditions.
But the point is this: to reject religion on the basis that it can
inspire violence would be rather like observing that all wars are
political acts and then concluding that politics should be rejected
as a result of this fatal flaw. That has been tried, on occasion, as
in the hippie communes of the sixties. It failed, as soon as the
idealists had to organize themselves. Politics and its associated
troubles returned, spontaneously. Similarly, the figure of the white
monk, Bernard of Clairvaux, preaching to the Crusade on the
hills of Vezelay, disturbs people today only because we live in an
age in which it seems possible to countenance excluding religion
from the public square, on the grounds that religion is inherently
violent. Except that if everyone has sacred values, then religiously
imagined violence – a preparedness to sacrifice – will always be
with us. Attacking Christianity or Islam as irrational is simply to
miss the point.

It also misses another, more hopeful facet of this
predicament. Perhaps because they implicitly recognize the link
between religion and violence, religious traditions have multiple
resources for resisting the turn to violence within them. One is
the Just War tradition. In varying forms, this proposes tests to see

whether waging war can be justified. The war must have a reasonable chance of succeeding, and its goals must be of greater goodness than the ills that war inevitably brings.

> *It is not until you know what you would die for that you also know what you would live for.*

'We had better acknowledge the sheer danger of religiousness', writes Rowan Williams, the Archbishop of Canterbury, in his reflection on the events of 9/11, *Writing in the Dust*. Williams was in Lower Manhattan on the day the twin towers fell; he witnessed it first-hand and could have died. His response is to recognize the evil and the acts that 'have to be confronted, taken forward, healed in the complex process of human history, always in collaboration with what we do and say and pray'. Which is to stress that religion may be dangerous, but it is simultaneously a way of confronting these threats.

There are also the exemplary lives of the founders of the great religions themselves. In Christianity, the tradition Rowan Williams inhabits, there is the example of Jesus. As the biblical stories have it, Jesus could become angry when his sacred values were confronted. He cast the money-changers out of the temple. He became angry with the Pharisees when they preferred to keep to the rules of the Sabbath rather than healing and saving a human life. The difference is that he did not seek to sacrifice them so as to preserve his profoundest convictions. Instead, he sacrificed himself by dying on the cross. It is a kind of reversal. It is as if Jesus says it is better to die than to kill in the name of religion.

Similar exemplary impetus is provided by the founders of other religious traditions too. In Islam, contemporary Salafi Muslims argue that before any individual wages violent jihad, they need to be purified. This is only to follow the pattern of the Prophet, who preached submission to Allah before picking up the sword. They then follow the general teaching with a specific observation: the world in which we live is one that can never be purified enough. It is *jahiliyya,* or ignorant. This has the net effect of delaying violent jihad indefinitely. Quintan Wiktorowicz has studied the impact of these teachings in his book *Global Jihad: Understanding September 11*. He quotes the Saudi Salafi scholar Muhammad al-Uthaymin, who decried the deployment of political turmoil: 'Let those who riot know that they only serve the enemies of Islam; the matter cannot be handled by uprising and excitement, but rather by wisdom.' Alternatively, another scholar, Muhammad Nasir al-Din al-Bani, warned,

> *The way to salvation is not, as some people imagine, to rise with arms against the rulers and to conduct military coups. In addition to being among contemporary bidahs [innovations], such actions disregard texts of Islam, among which is the command to change ourselves.*

We can conclude that religiosity becomes associated with violence because it is part of human nature to be violent. You can put that innate tendency down to the problem of giving meaning to the suffering that marks human experience. You can turn to evolutionary theory for an explanation. But whatever story you choose, the conclusion is the same: violence with a religious shape, because it includes the motif of sacrifice, will always be with us. But for the same reason, some of the most powerful forces against violence are found in religious traditions too, particularly in the lives of the individuals who founded them. Ultimately, religion seeks to contain inevitable violence, not perpetuate and celebrate it.

WHAT IS IT LIKE TO BE A FUNDAMENTALIST?

Radicalization, and why fundamentalism flourishes in an age of science

*R*ussell Razzaque *is a psychiatrist who works in London with patients confined on wards for the mentally ill. He is a Muslim, and whilst training in medicine he almost became a fundamentalist too.*

The path opened up to him during his university's freshers' week. At the annual jamboree showcasing clubs and organizations, he naturally headed for one stall marked 'The Islamic Society'. Why wouldn't he? He had already fallen in with a bunch of other Muslims, drawn together by such signals as backgrounds and turns of phrase, and also by the fact that so many of the activities during freshers' week seemed to involve drinking alcohol, often in substantial quantities, something of a problem for a Muslim.

He felt he might have found a home, which was welcome, as university was the first time he had found himself away from his family. He sensed that while university was an exciting place, because of the cosmopolitan mix of its students, it was also a place that precipitated feelings of vulnerability. The Islamic Society might help him feel energized by the melting pot, rather than simply lost in the melange.

When one of the leaders of the society started to talk about Islam, it struck Razzaque as unlike the religion he knew from his parents. The preaching repeatedly referenced the degeneracy of the West – its materialistic excesses, its colonial hubris. This seemed a bit odd, as the university that was offering them their education was embedded in the same Western culture. The speaker described a form of Islam that was focused on the unity of all Muslims, a universal brotherhood, an Islamic state or caliphate, where they could feel at home and restore the pride of Islam's historic golden past. Although it made Razzaque uneasy, the talk resonated with his feelings of vulnerability and being a little lost. He decided to return to hear what message might be delivered next week.

The preaching became more explicit, more incendiary. The rhetoric referenced the need for battle so that, inshallah, there might be a victory to restore Allah's rule upon Earth. The call was for all Muslims to do what Allah might ask, regardless of the price. One new student ventured an objection. He was used to debating in his mosque at home. Here, though, he was branded a *kafir*, an infidel, and silenced. There were good Muslims and he had shown himself to be a bad one.

Razzaque did not return to the Islamic Society the following week. Over the next few months, the society repeatedly tried to call and leaflet him, arguing that a true Muslim would stay with their group. He ensured that he steered clear of the circle, and the organization behind it, Hizb ut-Tahrir. But a decade later, post-9/11, after he had qualified and was working in a hospital, he became interested in the phenomenon of Islamic fundamentalism and its psychological appeal.

The roots of fundamentalism

Fundamentalism is found in all mainstream religions, though its modern form originated in Christianity (see *Will Science Put an End to Religion?*). A group of American Christians in the first half of the twentieth century decided that a list of tenets was required to act as the fundamental doctrines of faith, against which Christians could see clearly whether they were being faithful or backsliding, whether they were amongst the sheep or the goats.

There is good reason to assume that the emotional grip fundamentalism has on individuals is similar even in different religious contexts, though the way in which different fundamentalisms manifest themselves in practice is enormously diverse. In particular, only a small fraction of fundamentalists commit acts of violence – the atrocities with which the word has now become widely associated.

The emotional grip fundamentalism has on individuals is similar even in different religious contexts, though the way in which different fundamentalisms manifest themselves in practice is enormously diverse.

Having come so close to the broader phenomenon, having felt its allure, Razzaque has studied fundamentalism closely. He argues that, at base, fundamentalism appeals as a counterweight to a sense of alienation that people feel in response to life in the contemporary world. In his case, that estrangement took shape in an immigrant community, amongst the second generation. The parents of this generation were preoccupied with establishing a place for themselves and their families in their new home; among their children, all that was assumed, and so thoughts turned to what had been left behind and what had been lost. The pressures of modern life can be seen to pile up on the nuclear family unit, for example, whereas 'back home' there is an extended family, still embracing uncles and cousins, as well as mothers and children. That can make the older way of life seem pretty good by comparison.

Coupled to that is a sensitivity to being rejected amidst the rough and tumble of the massive, plural cities to which immigrant communities come. Vulnerable individuals can be very alert to unintended slights, which are in no way meant as deliberate persecution. Razzaque reports feeling this in relation to the social exclusion that unwittingly stemmed from not drinking alcohol.

His story can be generalized. The tale of migration and finding oneself in a culture with different habits and practices is part and parcel of the broader phenomenon of human mobility in a globalized world. As people shift from place to place, as they construct more pliable, less rooted patterns of life, what was once felt as solid melts in the air, to recall the comment of Karl Marx. The world is experienced as plastic, and one response is to insist upon a return to tangibles, to structures, to fundamentals – particularly in relation to religion. Those who self-consciously fight against the forces of modernity might come to think of themselves as the only true believers. They hold on to belief in order that belief might hold on to them.

Lines in the sand

The Jewish scholar Haym Soloveitchick has traced a different variation on this common theme amongst conservative Jewish communities such as the Orthodox and Haredi, in an essay entitled *Migration, Acculturation and the New Role of Texts*. A century or so ago, he begins, Jews inhabited a dual tradition that included both an intellectual engagement with the texts of the Jewish law and a practical tradition that learnt about the exercise of religion by a process of mimesis, imbibing a way of life passed on from the older to the younger generation, supported by being amongst friends. However, large-scale migration and immersion in the societal melting pot has disrupted the mimetic element. Children no longer live within extended families, and so don't breathe the same religious air.

> *The world is experienced as plastic, and one response is to insist upon a return to tangibles, to structures, to fundamentals – particularly in relation to religion.*

Younger generations may be forced, or feel compelled, to alter their inherited religious practices because they collide with the flexibility that secular modernity demands. How can you keep the Sabbath when the working week routinely demands that you work late on a Friday? There is a lot of pressure to stay in the office when all your colleagues stay late too.

The result is that the burden of Jewish observance falls on to the legal strand of the tradition and, having to bear the full weight of what it means to be a good Jew, it is strengthened by becoming legalistic, conservative, fundamentalist. Soloveitchick describes one vivid case in point, concerning the consumption of unleavened bread on Passover. Jewish law states that a minimal quantity, or *shiur*, must be eaten. The *shiur* is about the size of an olive, though for the first 2,000 years of this practice, little attention was paid to precisely how much it should be. 'One knew it automatically, for one had seen it eaten at one's parents' table on innumerable Passover eves; one simply did as one's parents had done', writes Soloveitchick.

Then, around the start of the Second World War, a well-known Talmudic scholar wrote a paper in which he used

THE MARTYRDOM OF SIX MEN AT BRAINFORD (1558) FROM JOHN FOXE'S BOOK OF MARTYRS. MODERN FUNDAMENTALISM IS SUBTLY DIFFERENT FROM THE LONG TRADITION OF PEOPLE WHO HAVE DIED FOR THEIR FAITH.

all his legal might and learning to question whether the size of olives was not much larger in Talmudic times, roughly around twice what scholars assumed now. 'He then insisted on a minimal standard about twice the size of the commonly accepted one', Soloveitchick explains. 'Within a decade his doctrine began to seep down into popular practice, and by now has become almost de rigueur in haredi circles.'

Before the twentieth century, the issue of *shiur* and other questions like it would have been considered theoretically interesting, though practically irrelevant; an element of religious gaming, almost fun. Now, though, in 'Jerusalem and Stamford Hill, London, in Borough Park, New York, and B'nai B'rak, Israel, religious observance is being both amplified and raised to new, rigorous heights', Soloveitchick writes. Instead of mimetic habits, the content of religion is filled with the strict performance of such specific gestures and codes. Similarly, certain details of belief may become the exclusive tokens by which an individual is judged as a true believer.

> *The fundamentalist mindset readily leads to a mentality that, first, feels at odds with the world, and then feels that the world is at odds with it.*

The shift is not limited to Judaism. In Christianity, a conservative or fundamentalist may feel that wearing a crucifix around her neck is absolutely non-negotiable. Another Christian may become sure that their stance on abortion, evolution or homosexuality is the major test of their convictions: any compromise on these issues represents the dissolution of their faith. They become lines in the sand that must not be crossed. Further, because it is in the very nature of a plural world to find yourself amidst individuals who do seek abortion, hold to evolution, or live with a partner of the same sex, the fundamentalist mindset readily leads to a mentality that, first, feels at odds with the world, and then feels that the world is at odds with it.

Texts are vitally important to the fundamentalist for the same reason. The kind of accuracy and security that fundamentalism offers can be secured through the Bible or the Qur'an. They are interpreted rigorously and narrowly, and are ascribed supreme positions in the faith: Christian fundamentalist creeds will often assert belief in the Bible before belief in God. Conversely, questioning the revealed word and subjecting it to modern critical methods is viewed as tantamount to blasphemy.

The fundamentalist mindset

Such alienation, and the corresponding turn to clear forms of faith, will be coloured by the particularities of a religion or set of historical circumstances. However, fundamentalisms are at root a product of the modern world itself, and so elements of the fundamentalist mindset might be felt by most people from time to time. We are talking about a contemporary existential predicament. In his witty and profound book *Lost in the Cosmos*, Walker Percy describes the feelings of many Americans, whether or not they have faith. The problem is that the scientific description of the universe dominates, and because it aims to be objective, it distances us from our engagement with the world around us, and so makes us unsure of our place in the universe:

> The lost self. . . *Every advance in an objective understanding of the Cosmos and in its technological control further distances the self from the Cosmos precisely in the degree of the advance so that in the end the self becomes a space-bound ghost which roams the very Cosmos it understands perfectly.*

Other aspects of secular life will play a part too. The historian of religion Diarmaid MacCulloch points to a feature that is often overlooked. Why, he asks, is the tone of religious expression in the world so often coloured by a reactionary and angry conservatism? He posits the possibility that shifting gender roles play a significant part because, as is often observed by sociologists of religion, the more extreme forms of conservative religion seem to have a direct appeal to educated but underemployed, energetic but frustrated young men. They become angry because the traditional roles that were allotted to them by virtue of being men, and which were sanctioned by religion, no longer exist. In *A History of Christianity*, MacCulloch speculates: '[The anger] embodies the hurt of heterosexual men at culture shifts which have generally threatened to marginalise them and deprive them of dignity, hegemony or even much usefulness.'

The more extreme forms of conservative religion seem to have a direct appeal to educated but underemployed, energetic but frustrated young men.

Whatever the causes, and they will be several, fundamentalist or conservative religion, in effect, attempts to come to the rescue. Its legalism seeks to create boundaries within which the individual

> *Science is essentially an exercise in reductionism: it seeks to understand the world by breaking it down into simpler chunks. Fundamentalism does much the same.*

may find personal sanctuary. If the external world is experienced as alienating and alienated, inside the warmth of the conservative group a sense of belonging and nurturing can be found. And there is another side to this too. For fundamentalists can, in fact, come to feel totally at home in the modern world, so long as their faith remains steady.

To put it another way, being a fundamentalist may well not be, primarily, frightening or disabling, as liberal observers might suppose. It can make for a happy existence, one in which the individual knows they are blessed, knows that they can survive in the world, knows who they are in the world.

Think of it like this. There is a kind of scientific attitude that is characteristic of fundamentalism, with its attention to the details of texts. Science is essentially an exercise in reductionism: it seeks to understand the world by breaking it down into simpler chunks. Fundamentalism does much the same. Instead of a religious way of life that springs from a complex and layered tradition, passed on by the subtle processes of mimesis, fundamentalists will ask for the evidence that supports this ritual or that belief.

This aspect of fundamentalism is supported by research showing that educated fundamentalists often study the sciences, and avoid the liberal arts. The precision of thought nurtured in, say, engineering feels not unlike the instructions by which the fundamentalist seeks to live, again with the attention to empirical details.

Alternatively, modern media such as the internet can serve the fundamentalist very well. The internet is nothing if not a written medium. It propagates words, and fundamentalists tend to put great store by the power of words. Their lifeblood is typically stirred by great preachers and teachers. They love the texts of their religious books. Little wonder that fundamentalists have shown themselves to be early adopters and swift masters of communications online.

The element of purity often associated with fundamentalism is not unlike the reductionist mentality too. Fundamentalists will often claim to be returning their religion to its original state, stripping away subsequent innovations and excessive cultural accretions. 'What would Jesus say?' asks the American Christian, as if he stands by his saviour at the lakeside in Galilee. One of the fastest-growing Muslim fundamentalist groups, the Salafis, believe that they have a direct connection to the first Companions of the Prophet because they share the same pure understanding of religion.

Militant atheism

It is sometimes observed that science is the only universal language that exists today. Newton's laws are the same in Sydney and the Swat valley; the quiet hand of evolution is shaping the natural world in the jungles of Indonesia and in the mountains of the American Bible Belt. Fundamentalism may reject elements of modern science, but the universalism promoted by science appeals in a deeper sense. Fundamentalism too promises a timeless, placeless and absolute version of the deepest truths that can be grasped by humankind.

The argument might be taken a step further. There has emerged, in recent decades, what is sometimes referred to as a militant form of atheism, individuals who seem as emotionally committed to science as the sole source of truth as fundamentalists might be to the documents of their faith. There is also a sense that this scientism is functioning as a way of bolstering the individual against the alienation of the modern world. As well as propagating the insights of science, it seems as important to atheists like Richard Dawkins to dispatch any alternatives. Alternatives are not merely perceived as implausible or ridiculous, but as threats to the progress of civilization (see *Will Science Put an End to*

Religion?). The atheist philosopher Julian Baggini argues that the atheism he aspires to entails values of open-mindedness. In his discussion of militant atheism in *Atheism: A Very Short Introduction*, he therefore concludes: 'Hostile opposition to the beliefs of others combined with a dogged conviction of the certainty of one's own beliefs is, I think, antithetical to such values.' All in all, religious fundamentalism and contemporary scientism are cultural cousins.

Fundamental instability

I am arguing that fundamentalism is a product of the modern world in several senses. At one level it is a reaction against the world and the forces destructive of mimetic traditions generated by globalization and pluralism. Refuge is sought in rigorous codes and practices, in strict tenets of belief. However, paradoxically, in defending itself against the world, it takes on some of the characteristics of the world, with its science-like attitude to faith.

Though only, we should add, to a degree. For fundamentalism is inherently unstable too. The external world pushes against the walls erected to protect the strongholds of faith. Like a life capsule in space surrounded by a vacuum, the fundamentalist bubble is vulnerable and liable to burst. Pressures on every side might cause it to rupture. The plural world offers endless alternatives that the next generation might choose. Fundamentalist elders know this, and so seek to control the education of their children in madrasas and colleges. Alternatively, if the faith is perpetuated by kin, as in Orthodox Jewish circles, there can be great pressure to marry within the close-knit group, and heavy sanctions are imposed on those who move out. Guards patrol the borders.

Fundamentalist enclaves are not the same as the older embedded faith cultures. They offer a relatively thin, legalistic air with which to nourish belief. When specifics and rules matter more than customs and habits, the character of the fundamentalist may become pernickety, disillusioned, and occasionally inflammatory. It is a brittle way of doing religion. This is an inherent part of what it is like to be a fundamentalist too.

WHAT IS BUDDHIST ENLIGHTENMENT?

Suffering, inner sanctuary, and whether Buddhism is supported by neuroscience

A*ged 29, the records tell us, the future Buddha, Siddhartha Gautama, left the home of his noble family. It must have been a happy youth: aristocratic privilege; an early marriage quickly followed by the birth of a son, suggesting love; and life in sight of the awesome heights of the Himalayas straddling the horizon, to inspire. The dream collapsed when he realized that it was all headed in one direction: sickness, corruption and death. Suffering was the underlying truth of existence. But why, why, why?*

Following the common Indian practice, Gautama set out on the road in pursuit of insight via the harsh habits of asceticism. 'When I saw a cowherd or one who was gathering wood, I fled from forest to forest, from valley to valley, from peak to peak.' The search for solitude, to deepen his reflections, continued for many years. It left him malnourished, parched and tormented. There was no enlightenment yet, though he had learnt something. Whatever the truth of suffering might be, the enforced suffering of ascetic practice does not unfold it. It merely compounds the suffering.

So he started to eat again, to look after his body, to return to health. His ascetical companions were shocked. This was sacrilege. He was insulting the hope for which they had sacrificed so long. Gautama was left alone.

One night he sat in stillness beneath the bodhi tree. The great awakening arrived. The philosopher Karl Jaspers describes it this way:

All at once a vision made everything clear to him: what is; why it is; how beings are caught up in blind lust for life; how they stray from body to body in a never-ending chain of rebirths; what suffering is, whence it comes, how it can be overcome.

The true path is a middle way, between ascetic denial and pleasurable indulgence. The Buddha's life itself demonstrates the route that it is necessary to follow. First there is the realization of suffering, the element that prompted him to leave home. Then there is the desire to understand, which drove him to a life on the road. Next comes a commitment to follow the path that will lead to understanding, which kept him on the path even when disillusioned. Finally comes understanding. The alienating horror of the first recognition is overcome at the end in the clear sight of the conditions of life, the very taste of wisdom. The path is a circle. The blind lust for life, also called attachment, is let go of when its emptiness is known. It is a kind of snuffing out, a nirvana.

> *Buddhist teachers will never tire of pointing out that the middle way is a subtle way, with many potential wrong turnings and misunderstandings.*

In a way, the experience is utterly mundane. 'When a monk breathes out long, he knows: I am breathing out long. Breathing in short, he knows: I am breathing in short', as one Buddhist scripture puts it. This is to act with full awareness, often now referred to as mindful attention. All is truly known, the Buddha continues,

When looking ahead and looking away, when flexing and extending his limbs, when wearing his robes and carrying his bowl, when eating, drinking and tasting, when defecating and urinating, when walking, standing, sitting, falling asleep, waking up, talking and keeping silent.

Nirvana follows from a disciplined curiosity about the texture of experience, which leads to 'the stilling of compulsions, the fading away of craving, detachment, stopping, nirvana'. Nirvana is not a peak experience, akin to the effects of psychotropic drugs. It is not a feat of endurance, as the yogis practised, when they were buried alive and yet survived, or starved themselves and yet lived. 'Something deep within Gotama seems to have stopped', reflects the Buddhist writer Stephen Batchelor. In *Confessions of a Buddhist Atheist* he writes:

> *He could remain fully present to the turbulent cascade of events without being tossed around by the desires and fears it evoked within him. A still calm lay at the heart of his vision, a strange dropping away of familiar habits, the absence, at least momentarily, of anxiety and turmoil . . .*

What is enlightenment?

Today, in the West, the story of the Buddha's discovery is relatively well known, though Buddhist teachers will never tire of pointing out that the middle way is a subtle way, with many potential wrong turnings and misunderstandings. If it were straightforward, a few hours under the bodhi tree would make enlightened beings of us all. But there is shocking aspect to this story.

At first, the Buddha thought he should tell nobody about his enlightenment. He remained under the tree and decided to keep silent – Sakyamuni, or the Silent One from Sakka, as one of his names describes him. It is said that at the moment of his awakening, the whole cosmos sang of the new-found freedom. 'The flowering trees bloomed; the fruit trees were weighed down by the burden of their fruit; the trunk lotuses bloomed on the trunks of trees.' But then the singing stopped. Suffering remained. The new Buddha knew that, in the same way that he had followed the path himself, that was the fate of every sentient creature. He could not do it for them. How could he even persuade them of the value of the path? As he had been in his youth, so most people were all their lives: they longed to be attached to the things that caused suffering. 'If I taught the way, people would not understand it and that would be exhausting and disappointing for me . . .'

So he decided to keep his secret to himself. That was the extent of his compassion, at least at first. The texts report that it was not until the Brahma appeared that the Buddha changed his mind. 'The world will be lost, the world will not have a chance', the god of creation pleaded.

It is as if, at the very inception of this great religion, there was an anxiety. What is enlightenment? Can it be communicated? How can it be known? It is a question that you hear repeated even now that Buddhism has become established in the West. What is the goal of Buddhism? Can I follow the same path?

I think part of the problem is one of language. After Buddhism first entered China, and then crept eastward towards Japan, it was several centuries before an authentic form of Buddhism took root, one that was right for these new places. It took that long for forms like Zen Buddhism and the Amidist schools to develop. Whilst there is a common essence to Buddhism, with its focus on suffering and its alleviation, it is as if there are multiple ways of describing what happens, of knowing what happens. This is presumably because it is only truly known in the experience of the individual, and the experience of each individual will be radically shaped by the specifics of their time, culture and place.

Translations of Buddhist texts have been available in the West for less than two centuries, the first serious engagement with them beginning in the nineteenth century when they were read by, for example, the philosophers Schopenhauer and Nietzsche. That is a relatively short period of time. Hence, today, the descriptions of the goal of the middle way seem various, confusing, elusive. The Buddha wondered whether it is really possible to teach the way. The old question has returned in the new, Western setting. How can it be answered?

The myth of materialism

As is always the case in spiritual communication, individuals who have tasted what is promised reach for existing languages to explore and communicate their understanding. Unsurprisingly, it is scientific discourse that is commonly resorted to in Western Buddhist circles. Neuroscientific discourse is a particular favourite.

Jeff Warren offers a helpful exploration of this route in his book *Head Trip: Adventures on the Wheel of Consciousness*. He imagines that Buddhists and other meditators are at the leading edge of the ongoing evolution of the brain, and that the aim is to cultivate and control your brain's capacities, rather than have your brain's whims and fancies cultivate you. 'It's all about flexibility', he writes:

> . . . *about slowly gaining control over the whole brain and then guiding its use with benevolent compassion, which [meditators] selectively boost . . . On this stage anything can be built: more compassion, more luminosity, greater understanding. And the frontal lobe – which houses the mechanisms of attention – is driving the whole shebang.*

Neuroscience is a way of talking that carries great weight and authority right now. That is to be expected. The ability to peer into the brain as it is firing is a very recent and remarkable feat. Discoveries are coming thick and fast. But it is wise to be wary of drawing speedy conclusions too.

Don't assume that the view science has of reality is always more true. Like any perspective, it has its strengths and weaknesses.

Take the philosopher Owen Flanagan's book, *The Bodhisattva's Brain: Buddhism Naturalized*. He argues that neuroscience allows meditators to strip away all the accretions that have gathered around Buddhism – the stuff about 'bodhisattvas flying on lotus leaves' – and see that at its heart there lies a philosophy of life that neuroscience knows to be true. The world is made only of matter and everything is determined, a perpetual trail of conditioned arising. Flanagan writes:

I believe that everything is impermanent, that everything (including my state of mind) is subject to the principles of cause and effect, and that given that I am among the things-that-there-are, I am impermanent and subject to the laws of cause and effect.

But beware. What Flanagan is actually doing is replacing the myths of the Indian subcontinent with the myths of the modern science lab.

Lest it be thought that deploying the word 'myth' in relation to science is insulting, I am in fact drawing on the title of a book by Paul Davies and John Gribbin, two leading cosmologists, called *The Matter Myth*. Myths are useful, in their time and place, and the myth of the materialist world view has been very useful as an assumption that has allowed science to proceed. But an assumption is not an absolute. It is just a convenient hypothesis. Further, the best myths reveal their limitations, they become their own undoing, because they point to the reality that lies beyond them. The materialist and determinist myths that underpin science have done the same, through the emergence of twentieth-century physics.

Werner Heisenberg, the leading quantum physicist, describes materialism as 'an extremely rigid frame for natural science which formed not only science but also the general outlook of the great masses of people'. In his book *Physics and Philosophy*, he continues:

This frame was so narrow and rigid that it was difficult to find a place in it for many concepts of our language that had always belonged to its very substance, for instance, the concept of mind, of the human soul or of life. Mind could be introduced into the general picture only as a kind of mirror of the material world.

It is a mechanical vision, in which phenomena like free will and subjective experience are reduced to physical and chemical processes. But by revolutionizing our understanding of the nature of matter, quantum theory dissolved the nineteenth-century view.

The rigid frame went too, or rather, it should go. (Scientific work in the biological sciences, such as neuroscience, often still deploys a nineteenth-century view of the world.) Atoms are not things, Heisenberg continues; they exist in a world of potentialities or possibilities rather than of objects or facts. So the materialist view, which views atoms as billiard balls in constant motion and collision, and the cosmos as conditioned arising, is incorrect.

Just what atoms are, quantum physics has not yet determined, for all its achievements in deriving precise equations describing what they do. In the meantime, Heisenberg recommends that individuals keep in touch with reality as they know and experience it, not least when discussing the ramifications of science. Welcome a dialogue between the two; stay open-minded. But don't assume that the view science has of reality is always more true. Like any perspective, it has its strengths and weaknesses. Nowhere is this more clear than with the conceptions that science questions of mind or soul or life or God.

Understanding the nature of enlightenment

In fact, traditional Buddhism views science as an incomplete way of knowing things, for the very reason that it is a reductionist way of knowing things. It sees that therein lies the power of science – it takes a specific stance towards the world – yet that is also a weakness. There are, therefore, some parallels between discoveries about the brain and what Buddhism teaches about the nature of the mind. But there is one crucial aspect of human experience that science cannot touch, though it is the very path that the Buddha advised his followers to develop. Introspection. The techniques of meditation and phenomenological investigation. Brain science is condemned to remain on the outside, looking in, whereas the human individual can directly inspect the contents of their mind. That is what it is to be self-aware. It is possible to be confused and deluded. We will be confused and deluded. But that is only to say the path is hard, the training long.

The power of introspection also explains how the Buddha, whose world did not contain brain scanners, managed to discover

> *Traditional Buddhism views science as an incomplete way of knowing things, for the very reason that it is a reductionist way of knowing things.*

insights about the life of the mind that have sustained countless individuals for two and a half millennia. Shakespeare has achieved the same timeless reflections on matters of love. Augustine, the philosopher bishop of the fourth century, can hardly be beaten on the human experience of time (see *What is the Literal Meaning of Scripture?*). Brain science, for all its insights, changes its mind almost every week.

There are other discourses that Western Buddhists deploy to understand the nature of enlightenment. They work better, to my mind, because they follow the path that Heisenberg advised. Rather than seeking the authority of science, they take note of the science, and rest in the authority of lived experience.

The author Peter J. Conradi deploys the notion of emptiness, in his book *Going Buddhist: Panic and Emptiness, the Buddha and Me.* The concept of emptiness generally has negative connotations in the West, he warns. But in the East it signifies not nothing, but a kind of free openness.

Later, when you have gained some experience in the process of liberating thoughts, they are said to undo themselves as a snake might untie a knot in its own body.

This openness begins when it is noticed that feelings such as anger or pride do not have to lead you down a vicious spiral of tight feeling. The habit might be checked, to a degree, just by examining the insubstantial nature of bad thoughts. They come and go, but needn't automatically breed one after another. Conradi continues: 'Finally, a third stage, you master the liberation of thoughts, which can now, like a thief in an empty house, no longer cause harm.'

Another writer on Buddhism is the religious scholar Karen Armstrong. She uses an analogy with a deeper sense of their being upon which creative people draw. This is a place inside that allows the artist or poet to engage with the world with an attitude that is detached but genuine, observing and engaged. And it is not just creative sorts who need this inner core. Everyone does, in fact, otherwise life tends to fall apart. So nirvana, for Armstrong, is a 'still centre' that yields such meaning.

Once a person has learned to access this nucleus of calm, he or she is no longer driven by conflicting fears and desires, and is able to face pain, sorrow and grief with equanimity. An enlightened or awakened human being has discovered a strength within that comes from being correctly centered, beyond the reach of selfishness.

A combination of these two descriptions seems close to how Western Buddhists are now redescribing Nirvana for the twenty-first-century condition. It is not deterministic, though it recognizes the contingencies of life. It is not materialist, acknowledging the primacy of mind. It incorporates notions of psychological well-being: the ability to face fears, vulnerabilities and desires and not be spontaneously driven by them. It accesses a way of being that reduces the gap between reality as it is and the way things often appear to us, distorted. It is sane, calm, creative.

Changing your view of the world

So can you and I be enlightened? I imagine that most people have tasted enlightenment, if momentarily, perhaps when caught unawares. There is a story that the Buddha himself had a fleeting glimpse of it when he was still a boy. He was sitting under the shade of a rose-apple tree and caught sight of a freshly ploughed field. Spontaneously, he saw it quite clearly. He observed the cut grass. He spotted insects that had been killed and disturbed. It was no longer a farmer's field, but a whole cosmos of activity, life, destruction, carnage. It was as if he observed from a place beyond good and evil. He could see everything as it was. Later, he recognized that that moment had been an anticipation of his subsequent great awakening.

All the Buddhist seeks to do, in a way, is to extend what is for most a passing puddle of peace into a deep pool of awareness.

And yet there is something that remains beyond description, something about the experience itself that cannot be caught in words. It is ineffable. Like describing the smell of coffee, you need to deploy words and metaphors that only work when the person who hears them knows about the smell of coffee already. It is a bit like the response Louis Armstrong made when asked what jazz might be: 'If you still have to ask . . . shame on you.'

The psychologists Fraser Watts and Philip Barnard have proposed that human beings have two cognitive systems. One is propositional, reflective, articulate, scientific. It enjoys conversations that say 'This can be explained . . .' or 'The truth is that . . .' The second is implicational, pre-reflective, experiential. This cognitive system is deployed when individuals know, say, that they are seeing the colour red or that they love their children. If you asked them to prove or discuss these experiences, they might find that difficult. They might even find the request offensive. The implicational handles our background assumptions, the frame through which we see the world.

Buddhism is asking us to attend to our implicational system more than the propositional. The latter loves to be questioned, tested, challenged. But the implicational, because it feels like the ground upon which we stand, is more resistant. It is very hard to shift. To be enlightened, though, is to have questioned, tested and challenged it. When that happens, you do not just accumulate more knowledge. Your whole view of the world is changed.

IS CONFUCIANISM A RELIGION?

The philosophy that thrives in the world's most populous country

*H*aving *been suppressed for much of the twentieth century, religion is thriving again in China. The 'new' faiths of Christianity and Islam are doing well. So are the indigenous traditions of Daoism and Confucianism. So what, then, does Confucius say?*

It was a cold morning in Beijing. We had stepped out to walk in Tiantan Park, which surrounds the Temple of Heaven. The air was crisp, the sky blue, the temperature several degrees below zero. The place was packed with early birds. Folk were practising t'ai chi in formation. Some were playing games with bats and balls. One man hung by his knees from a tree, apparently attending to his breathing. The mood was not rowdy. It felt focused.

Then, every so often, I noticed upright bollards, housing speakers, emerging from the grass or concrete. As you approached, you could catch a quiet sound like chanting emanating from them. I later gathered that the words being spoken were those of Confucius. I could not understand what he was saying. But it struck me as a powerful metaphor that in Tiantan Park, his words infused the air.

Confucius' life

Confucius was born about 2,500 years ago – a generation before Socrates, two or three centuries after the prophets of the Hebrew Bible. His world was a turbulent one. Historians refer to it as the Chunqiu, the 'Spring and Autumn' period, though that makes it sound tranquil when in fact it was brutalized by constant sparring between warlords. The settled life of the village was continually under threat.

Confucius, or Master Kung as the name means, experienced the unrest directly and personally. The story has it that he was an answer to his parents' prayers for a child, though the joy of the miracle did not last. His aristocratic father died when he was three and, losing almost everything, his mother was forced to raise him in poverty. As a child, he grew enamoured with ritual and was remembered for liking to play with the sacrificial vessels. They might have held out the promise of pattern and meaning in an otherwise inchoate and humiliating world. Perhaps he became withdrawn too: we are told that he married, and though he had three children, the relationship was loveless.

At the age of 19, he went into service with a noble family, and worked for the manager of their parks. He studied ritual with the Daoist master Lao Dan, and by the time he was 32, he was instructing young gentlemen as part of their training for government service. A year or so later, he made his way to the imperial capital, Lu – in present day south-east Shandong – an important centre of religion. His aim was to retrieve the customs of the Chou empire, which had broken up because of the warring. A year later, he had to flee the capital. The legend has it that he learnt to play music, an activity that so absorbed him, he often forgot to eat. Later, he was able to return to Lu and spent 15 years in study.

Book X of Confucius' *Analects*, or memories of conversations, is traditionally regarded as biographical. It offers a number of sketches of the man, probably idealized, though through the myth can be detected a person with the kind of steady character that does not vary, regardless of who is they are talking to.

When at court conversing with the officers of a lower grade, he is friendly, though straightforward; when conversing with officers of a higher grade, he is restrained but precise. When the ruler is present he is wary, but not cramped.

That humility was reflected in his conversation.

Confucius, at home in his native village, was simple and unassuming in manner, as though he did not trust himself to speak. But when in the ancestral temple or at Court he speaks readily, though always choosing his words with due caution.

Physically, he must have been a large man: 'On entering the Palace Gate he seems to contract his body, as though there were not sufficient room to admit him', the *Analects* remarks.

His abilities were finally recognized properly around the age

PORTRAIT OF CONFUCIUS

of 50, when he was appointed to various ministerial posts of increasing responsibility. But then trouble struck again, and he had to go back into exile. (Another story says that the prince of Lu was sent a troupe of 80 dancing girls by his rival, which so distracted him that he became lackadaisical about his duties and ignored the advice of Confucius.)

Confucius travelled for about 12 years, accompanied by his disciples, a group probably numbering about 70. They faced many dangers and threats as they searched for employment, though mainly they were met with repeated indifference and apathy from those who might have benefited from his wisdom. Confucius is said to have cried out, 'Let me go home, let me go home.' But as was said of another wandering sage, a prophet is not welcome in his own home town.

Finally, aged 68, he returned to Lu, where he wrote poetry lamenting the years wasted meandering through the nine states. He refused to return to any political post, though he was later referred to as a man who should have been king. And then, the meaning of his life became clearer. 'Is that not the man who knows that striving is without hope and yet goes on?' a hermit observed one day. Confucius' greatest achievement was his faithfulness, his persistence. Now, he studied the *I Ching*, tidied up the annals of his times, and wrote about education.

He recognized that death was approaching when one day he took a stroll in the garden, singing these words: 'The great mountain must collapse, the mighty beam must break and the wise man wither like a plant.' His students were alarmed. Confucius lay down. Eight days later he was dead, at the age of 72, though this number is a magical one in Chinese literature and so is more symbolic than factual.

Turning to the past

Confucius is one of the figures associated with the Axial Age, an extended period in history when the world seemed to turn on its axis. Jesus, the Buddha, Socrates and the Hebrew prophets are the others, and their lives are similar in so far as they lived in frighteningly troubled periods of history, an experience that precipitated great insights into the human condition. Karl Jaspers, the philosopher who coined the term 'Axial Age', summed up Confucius' basic idea in a phrase that is almost a motto: the renewal of antiquity. Jaspers explains that 'His fundamental questions were: What is the old? How can we make it our own? How can we make it a reality?' They are questions for periods of history confronted by change.

Confucius saw history through the verities of the present and thereby instilled a new consciousness of ritual and tradition.

The irony is that this way of treating the past was new. Confucius saw history through the verities of the present and thereby instilled a new consciousness of ritual and tradition. This was not to be followed blindly, however; it was to be conducted with a conscious, aware attitude. That way the past is transformed by the present. His early love of ritual was not a form of escape; it represented a pathway into life.

But why turn to the past at all, we might ask – we who are indoctrinated with the dream of progress, who believe that it is the future that should shape the present, not the past? The great advantage that the past has is that it saves us from ourselves. The past was before we were, and therefore it is free of our prejudices and ignorance. The future, though, depends upon us because it comes from us. Not only does that mean we will pass our failings on to the future, but the future can become a great burden too, as if the meaning of our lives depends solely upon us – upon our successes at work, in our creativity, through our children. We may have some successes. We will surely know many failures. But these might be understood, or mitigated, by having them judged according to the wisdom of the ages, rather than attempting to root them in the as yet unreal and fantastical future.

> *The aim is not simply to repeat. It is to sustain what is true.*

People in the past had prejudices and were ignorant too, but we can see that clearly, if we look carefully and critically. What we can't see are our own prejudices and blind spots, unless we contrast our present with their past, when our ignorance may come to light. So this is history as a source of lessons, not as a process of imitation. 'A man born in our days who returns to the ways of antiquity is a fool and brings misfortune upon himself.' The aim is not simply to repeat. It is to sustain what is true. Jaspers describes the process in this way:

> *This is done by learning, which means not merely to acquire information about something but to make it our own . . . Without learning, all other virtues are obscured as though by a fog and*

degenerate: without learning, frankness becomes vulgarity; bravery, disobedience; firmness, eccentricity; humanity, stupidity; wisdom, flightiness; sincerity, a plague.

This teaching has practical ramifications. Confucius was against the hereditary principle, for example. The problem with a son winning the crown is that the proof of the worthiness of the son lies in the future. Again, that is entirely unknown. Better, then, to pass rule on to the best men of the present age. It was in no small part because China had become wedded to the hereditary principle that she found itself constantly racked by war and strife, Confucius diagnosed.

A way of life

Confucianism can be said, perhaps controversially, to be a religion in several ways. First, it involves ritual and practices. Take Confucius' interest in the *I Ching*, the *Book of Changes*. This is an ancient document for divination, comprised of sets of oracular statements. Just how it works depends on who you ask. Some would say it is through spirits. Others out of sheer delusion.

The psychologist Carl Jung's interpretation might resonate well with Confucius' more mainstream philosophy. In an introduction to the *I Ching*, written for the translation by the Sinologist Richard Wilhelm, Jung argued that the book brings together subjective and objective views of the world, and forces the individual to interpret the clash that results, thereby encouraging them to 'outgrow' their problem. It is not that the problem is solved. It is seen with a new perspective. 'Some higher or wider interest arose on the person's horizon, and through this widening of his view the insoluble problem lost its urgency', Jung explains. 'What, on a lower level, had led to the wildest conflicts and panicky outbursts of emotion, viewed from the higher level of the personality, now seemed like a storm in the valley seen from a high mountain-top.' Unsurprisingly, Jung reads the *I Ching* as a therapist, though like Confucius' view of history, he discerns the same value: it clears the mists of our immediate concerns and orientates us in a direction that is rooted in a deeper, more ancient truth.

Confucianism also offers a way of life, insisting that following this way of life is where life's best satisfaction is to be found. This aspect of its philosophy is communal. 'A man cannot live with the birds and beasts', Confucius says. 'If I do not live with men, with whom shall I live?' Further, this communal living is not for companionship's sake. It is because the heart of the human condition is collective. Nowhere is this demonstrated more starkly than in the ideogram for the nature of man, *jên*. It means 'man' and 'two'; thus, to be human is to be with others. 'He who is concerned only with the purity of his own life ruins the great human relations.'

Jên is fleshed out in a number of ways. Relationships between individuals are of supreme importance. 'Do not display to your inferiors what you hate in your superiors. Do not offer your neighbours on the left what you hate in your neighbours on the right.' This is not just because it is good to be nice; it is because we are all in it together. 'The lover of mankind strengthens men, for he himself wishes to be strengthened; he helps men toward success, for he himself wishes to achieve success.'

That said, not all people are the same. The strength of humankind is found in its diversity, because each person will embody different virtues according to their age, development and stage. Together we are more than the sum of our parts. Similarly, each age of man comes with its own vices.

> *The strength of humankind is found in its diversity, because each person will embody different virtues according to their age, development and stage.*

> *In youth when the vital forces are not yet developed, guard against sensuality; in manhood, when the vital forces have attained their full strength, against quarrelsomeness; in old age, when the forces are on the wane, against avarice.*

Confucius also taught something akin to Aristotle's doctrine of the mean, that true virtue is found in between

143

extremes. The best state an individual might strive for is in between hope and anger, in between grief and joy. Again like Aristotle's notion of practical intelligence, Confucius argues that this mean can only be discovered in life, not in theory. Virtue is experienced or felt when properly known and understood. You know *jên* when you see it, in the sage. Conversely, to those who don't know it by acquaintance, virtue may seem naive or mysterious. 'Nothing is more obvious than what is secret, nothing more evident than what is most hidden.'

There is another aspect to this 'secret', namely that its wisdom is dependent upon circumstances. Confucius is in no doubt that there is such a thing as Truth, with a capital 'T'. However, Truth is greater than the human capacity to grasp it in its entirety, and so no dogmatic statement or credal summary will ever quite do. 'The superior man is not absolutely for or against anything in the world. He supports only what is right.' Confucius was a philosopher who spoke in relative terms, not absolutes, because he respected the absolute. When he did not understand something, he did not equivocate, for such caginess is likely to lead people astray. Better to indicate a lack of knowledge on the matter and hold back.

Know your limits

This attitude raises the third way in which Confucianism can be thought of as a religion. Confucius was supremely aware of his limits.

'To present what you know as knowledge and what you do not know as ignorance: that is knowledge.' We might call it being Socratic – Socrates, Confucius' fellow Axial sage, being the Greek who realized that the key to wisdom is not the accumulation of facts, but as profound an appreciation as is possible of the edges of your sight. It is like living on the circumference of a circle. The inside of the circle represents what you know, the outside of the circle what you do not know. Living on the edge is where someone should aspire to be, as then they can feel both at home in the world and perpetually astonished by it. They can see in and gaze out.

Confucius' appreciation of limits also embraced a clear recognition of the inevitable failures of human beings. The problem is not that the world is inherently evil. If that were so, he would not be able to rely on the past to cast light on the present. It is that people have faults, often profound. 'That good predispositions are not cultivated, that what men have learned is not effectual, that men know their duty and are not drawn to it, that men have faults and are unable to correct them: these are things that grieve me.' This lack of sanctity he took to include himself, so that when his disciples were, on occasion, shocked at his flaws, he asked them why they were distressed. In his view, although there have been saints, they lived long ago.

> *Living on the edge is where someone should aspire to be, as then they can feel both at home in the world and perpetually astonished by it. They can see in and gaze out.*

He believed that ignorance precluded discussion of many subjects that so fascinate the religious of the West. The nature of virtue, the determinism of fate, the pursuit of happiness, the inevitability of death: the trouble with such questions is that they are liable to draw you away from the here and now. They seduce theologians and sceptics alike because they surreptitiously offer an escape from the issue that is most pressing: what next, what now? In addition, they are subjects that admit little useful reflection, as the answers are largely unknown, ineffable. 'If you do not know life, how should you know death?'

'Though such an attitude many be put down to agnosticism', Jaspers continues, 'it does not signify indifference to the unknowable, but rather a reverence which is unwilling to transform intimation into pseudo knowledge or lose it in words.' Instead, Confucius practised the traditional religions, and did not bother to question the reality of omens. In this sense, he was conservative. There is clear benefit in remembering the ancestors; in your birth, they initiated you into the flow of life, so you do well to keep open the channels of energy they offer. And anyway, religious traditions carry the distillation of thousands of years, so why would one individual believe they can seriously challenge them? Better to use them. On one occasion he pointed to the palm of his hand and remarked, 'One who knew the meaning of the great sacrifice would be able to rule the world as easily as to look here.'

There is one final sense in which Confucius is an inspirer of a religious way of life. In his own lifetime, he was something of a failure, if being well known and followed is the measure of success.

Troubled times such as his precipitate many possible responses. Jesus can be said to have responded to the turbulence of first-century CE Judea with the preaching of an apocalyptic prophet. Socrates responded to the bloody rises and falls of Athens' golden age by developing the way of life called philosophy. But the reason Confucius is remembered is because of the politics that followed his death.

Over 200 years later, his teaching did become widespread when it was adopted by the Han dynasty. It was a bureaucratic state, and Confucius' worldly ethos, coupled with the stories of his life, were used to sustain and grow the bureaucracy. State power twisted the original teaching to its own, peculiar ends, of course. Learning so as to make something your own morphed into learning by rote. Respect for the past because it challenges the present became respect for the past because it preserves the present.

The magnificent edifices that followed Jesus and Socrates achieved the same transformation. Institutionalized religions and philosophies conceal as much as they reveal about their original teachings, their first animating spirits. That too is an important lesson for the followers of the great religions.

IS NATURE DIVINE?

Animism, ecology, and the struggle to participate with nature

*T*he way the modern mind looks at the world conceals some aspects of nature as much as it reveals others. It views the world through lenses that brilliantly spot its mechanical and deterministic functions, everything from the dynamics of a bird in flight to the force on an apple falling from a tree. But this reductionism overlooks the systemic, integrated aspects of life. Gaia: the view that the Earth as a whole is a living organism.

The ecologist David Abram's particular interest is in the world of shamans, those healers who have the ability to cure by visualizing disease as an imbalance or a malevolent presence in the body. 'The primacy to the magician of nonhuman nature – the centrality of his relation to other species and to the earth – is not always evident to Western researchers. Countless anthropologists have managed to overlook the ecological dimension of the shaman's craft, while writing at great length of the shaman's rapport with "supernatural" entities', he reflects in *The Spell of the Sensuous*, continuing, 'that which is regarded as mysterious, powerful, and beyond human ken must therefore be of some other, non-physical realm above nature, "supernatural"'. The practice of offering gifts to spirits, as is widespread in traditions from indigenous animism to the Shintoism of Japan, is regarded as mere superstition.

But Abram has come to see more in these activities, and it has to do with a recovery of the systemic, integrated nature of the world.

He recalls once staying in a Bali village, where his host had prepared several platters, a few inches long, holding small mounds of white rice. She then carefully placed the offerings around the periphery of the compound. Abram gained a first, Western-style insight into the apparently odd practice the next morning, when he saw that ants were carefully offloading the rice kernels and carrying them back to their nests. That is one explanation: offer some rice to the ants outside, and they might not help themselves to the rice in your home.

But why did his host refer to the ants as spirits, when they were clearly ants? Did she think of them as spirits? 'My encounter with the ants was the first of many experiences suggesting to me that the "spirits" of an indigenous culture are primarily those modes of intelligence or awareness that do *not* possess a human form.' One example is the spirit/intelligence of ants.

Think of it this way. The famous naturalist David Attenborough recently returned to Madagascar to make a film about the island, having first done so 50 years previously. He had with him his diaries from that earlier trip, and on occasion read out excerpts from them to camera.

One day, he related, he had been observing a family of indri, the large lemurs that live on Madagascar. 'Once we saw a young male join a young female, sitting behind her, his legs stretched out on either side of her', he read out. 'They licked and embraced one another for half an hour. Then suddenly a bird screeched loudly and startlingly. Immediately the male put a protective and reassuring arm around her. It was most touching to see.' He reflected that he had been deeply moved to observe this spontaneous sharing of affection. Then he looked directly into the camera. 'Hmm!' he spluttered, with a disparaging smile. 'Anthropomorphism run riot! But there you are, that's what I wrote.'

It is an ingrained scientific habit. For good reason, science is wary of anthropomorphism. It seeks an objective point of view. But what a shame that it dismisses what the subjective, experiential view might have to say too. That is to lose a different kind of wisdom, to trounce it with the sort that is acceptable. We know the satisfaction of sipping cool water on a hot day. Do we know what it is like for the hungry humming bird to sip sweet nectar? We know what it is like to pant after an exhilarating climb. Do we know what it

> *For good reason, science is wary of anthropomorphism. It seeks an objective point of view.*

is like for the mountain goat to leap up the hillside? We do, and perhaps they can tell us more than we know too.

A living landscape

Respect for that other wisdom, the intelligence and awareness that is related to ours but takes non-human form, is the reason why the Balinese woman referred to the ants as spirits. 'To humankind, these Others are purveyors of secrets, carriers of intelligence that we ourselves often need', continues Abram, now understanding more deeply. 'It is these Others who can inform us of unseasonable changes in the weather, or warn us of imminent eruptions and earthquakes, who show us, when foraging, where we may find the ripest berries or the best route to follow back home.' In fact, the animal with which Western human beings have the most intimate, affectionate relationship – the dog – is now respected as an Other who can act as eyes for the blind, as a warning for the epileptic and, I heard recently, of forthcoming earthquakes too.

How these canine feats are achieved is a good question. Intelligence, smell, magnetic resonance? But that they can be useful, and that human beings gain from their relationship with the intelligence of creatures, might be said to be an insight that is returning to Western consciousness after many years.

The respect for spirits in aboriginal cultures does not stop there. It is properly animistic. It embraces the belief that not just animals but plants and inanimate objects have souls like human beings too. They all possess modes of intelligence. This is something that is at risk of being lost.

A Spirit House on Jong Kham Lake in Mae Hong Son, Thailand. Asian spiritual houses embody modern animism.

It is not just the fault of objective science. Animism can be thought of as at the opposite end of the scale from the Judaeo-Christian view of things. Christianity has sometimes taught that only human beings have souls, as only human beings are made in the image of God – or to put it in more secular language, only human beings have full self-conscious awareness, a sense of being a person with a present, past and future. The limiting of soulfulness to *Homo sapiens* is now often challenged by scientists and philosophers who have become convinced that it makes sense to refer to at least some other animals as having personhood, to a degree. Candidates include primates, pigs and members of the crow family. Aristotle, too, argued that all animate creatures have souls, the soul being the aspect of the flower or the tree that makes them self-moving, not dissimilarly to birds and bees, just more slowly. But he didn't go so far as to include inanimate things, like mountains or rivers.

Animism does. It has a view of ecological wholeness that means the spirits move in between the animate and inanimate. Abram writes:

> The 'body' – human or otherwise – is not yet a mechanical object. It is a magical entity, the mind's own sensuous aspect, and at death the body's decomposition into soil, worms, and dust can only signify the gradual reintegration of one's elders and ancestors into the living landscape, from which all, too, are born.

The air surrounding us can be envisaged as carrying a subtle echo of the presence of the dead, until the spirit finds its new home. Such a belief informs the practice of cremation. Burning a corpse transforms it into the elemental substances – smoke or air, fire, and ash or earth – which hastens the return to the earth, ensuring that the spirit won't trouble the living for longer than necessary.

There are myriad forms and myths in animism, reflecting the strong sense of connection to particular places. A nearby volcano will inform the beliefs of those who live alongside it, the fiery mountain carrying a spirit to be engaged with quite as fully as the ants in the Balinese village.

Animism can be thought of as at the opposite end of the scale from the Judaeo-Christian view of things.

An important point is that animism does not invoke spirits to explain things. That is another scientific assumption, as if primitive cultures don't understand why the lightning jumps or the thunder claps, though they long to, and so try to explain what is going on by invoking the anger of gods, say. But this seems to be a misunderstanding. What it assumes is that people who live without the benefit of a scientific mindset are frustrated proto-scientists, the difference between us and them being that they are unfortunate enough to live without knowledge of the great breakthroughs of Galileo and Newton, of Boyle and Harvey. We are the lucky ones, living in the light of their discoveries.

Instead, though, it is more likely that non-scientific civilizations just didn't ask scientific questions, or at least, they didn't ask them with the same force. They were not so interested in how they might explain phenomena. What engaged them was where they belonged in nature, what was their place. They did not think to control nature, but to respect and learn from it. Animism is, therefore, one way of attending to and revering non-human powers. For good and ill, it is simply unlike the scientific attempt to bring natural forces within the ambit of human control. Instead it seeks a kind of harmony, which is why it so appeals to ecologists.

Shifting perspectives

There are fascinating intimations of the transition from the animist point of view to the scientific in various literary texts of the Renaissance, a period that can, in some ways, be understood as one that tried to incorporate both perspectives. For example, King Lear, in Shakespeare's play, rages against the weather, seeing in the cracks and howls of the thunder and lightning a reflection of his daughters' betrayal. On one level he knows that the elements are not rebelling against him, as he thinks his daughters are. He knows the weather cannot be accused of unkindness, as he believes of his children. But on another level, nature still seems to mirror his own distress. In this modernized text Lear yells:

> *So go ahead and have your terrifying fun. Here I am, your slave – a poor, sick, weak, hated old man. But I can still accuse you of kowtowing, taking my daughters' side against me, ancient as I am. Oh, it's foul!*

The more scientific view is, ironically, represented in the play by the King's Fool. He is the practical one, and advises the distraught monarch to go indoors.

> *Oh, uncle, it's better to smile and flatter indoors where it's dry than get soaked out here. Please, uncle, let's go in and ask your daughters to forgive you. This storm has no pity for either wise men or fools.*

In the play, you get both perspectives. The King's speaks powerfully to the soul. The Fool's speaks sensibly about more practical concerns, like keeping dry. Both are important matters.

Alternatively, there is the ascent of Mont Ventoux made by the Renaissance humanist Petrarch. It is sometimes said that he was the first person who thought to climb a mountain simply for the pleasure of it, giving birth to the sport of mountaineering. That has been questioned. But what is of note is his response to the experience. It seems to capture this shift between Other-concern and self-concern.

The story goes that Petrarch climbed the mountain, and later wrote about the feat in a letter to his friend, the monk

Dionigi di Borgo San Sepolcro. Admiring nature's grandeur, and stirred by the view from high up in the Alps, he reached into his pocket and read from Augustine's *Confessions*. It was a daily habit, only this time it prompted a very different response to the scenery.

His eyes caught these words: 'People are moved to wonder by mountain peaks, by vast waves of the sea, by broad waterfalls on rivers, by the all-embracing extent of the ocean, by the revolutions of the stars. But in themselves they are uninterested.' Augustine was writing many centuries before, though he too is often credited with the first stirrings of an objective attitude towards the self: his *Confessions* can be thought of as the first introspective autobiography. This different sensibility is what Petrarch noticed. Should he be wasting his time admiring the heights? What could he learn from them? Should he not be contemplating the state of his soul? He wrote to Dionigi:

> *I closed the book, angry with myself that I should still be admiring earthly things who might long ago have learned from even the pagan philosophers that nothing is wonderful but the soul, which, when great itself, finds nothing great outside itself. Then, in truth, I was satisfied that I had seen enough of the mountain; I turned my inward eye upon myself . . .*

The insights of animism

David Abram believes we live in an age that is so interested in itself that it is at risk of destroying the natural world upon which that self still depends. He argues that there is something vital to be regained from the animistic way of viewing the world, and recommends becoming 'a student of subtle differences'. He himself noticed a shift in his senses. A presence reported in a house came to mean something to him; he could not just put it down to a trick of the light. He heard birds singing and thought the noise not just the inventive product of aeons of evolution, but a meaningful mode of communication akin to his

> *We live in an age that is so interested in itself that it is at risk of destroying the natural world upon which that self still depends.*

own. He started to have extraordinary encounters with monkeys and lizards, sharing with them a mutual curiosity.

It was as if my body were suddenly being motivated by a wisdom older than my thinking mind, as though it was held and moved by a logos, deeper than words, spoken by the Other's body, the trees, the air, and the stony ground on which we stood.

This is all valuable, necessary intelligence. It's what the Balinese woman knew.

What is striking about Abram is not only that he is a scientist who opens his mind to the insights of animism, but he is a trained magician too. He understands how people can be fooled and deluded. He describes weighing up his conjuring abilities against the abilities of the shamans he meets. And yet that does not lead him to debunk animism, as sceptics do. Instead, it gives him a deeper respect for it.

Abram is one of a growing band of scientifically informed individuals who are starting to see nature in such ways, and are not afraid to talk about it either. Another is the botanist Diana Beresford-Kroeger. In her book *40 Ways Trees Can Save Us*, she notices the parallels between the mystical qualities ascribed to the colours red and green since ancient times, and the extraordinary function of red haemoglobin in blood and green chlorophyll in plants revealed by biology. Just as holly was holy to the Celts because of its evergreen leaves and red berries, so haemoglobin and chlorophyll have been marked as 'sister molecules' by science. Haemoglobin is the molecule that transports oxygen into organisms. Chlorophyll is the molecule that transports oxygen out of organisms. They work in almost identical, though opposite, ways. 'It seems like part of a divine plan, these twin sister molecules working hand-in-hand in their quantum homes to forge life for the entire planet.' Both perspectives can be incorporated.

Another common source of such inspiration comes from those who work with primates, particularly the scientists

who spend long periods of time observing them in the wild.
Jane Goodall is a pioneer, ascribing minds and personalities to
the chimpanzees amongst whom she lived. She transgressed that
scientific taboo, of becoming emotionally involved with them, of
anthropomorphizing them. She also talks openly of her mystical
experiences with them. 'The longer I spent on my own, the more
I became one with the magic forest world that was now my home',
she writes in *In the Shadow of Man*. 'Inanimate objects developed
their own identities and, like my favourite saint, Francis of Assisi, I
named them and greeted them as friends. "Good morning, Peak," I
would say as I arrived there each morning.'

Goodall argues that the divide between
human and other, between subjective and objective,
is unnecessary. It is perfectly possible to do good
science and experience such profound connections
with nature. 'How sad that so many people seem
to think that science and religion are mutually
exclusive', she continues. She celebrates both the
outstanding achievements of the human mind in understanding the
natural world, and the extraordinary experience that the mind can
appreciate when it is open to mystery and awe. 'How sad it would be
… if our left brains were utterly to dominate the right so that logic
and reason triumphed over intuition and alienated us absolutely from
our innermost being, from our hearts, our souls.'

> *The appeal of animism is that it speaks of the divine in nature.*

The primatologist Birute Galdikas is another pioneer. (It
is interesting that these three are all women.) An authority on
orang-utans, she has made the fascinating observation that gardens
and forests seem frequently to be reflected in the buildings and
mythologies of great religions. In Islam, paradise is depicted as a
garden. In Christianity, gothic architecture mirrors the patterns
of the forest, with long shafts of light descending from dappled
heights and dancing amidst slender trunks or columns. There must
be something ancient and remembered in the mirroring.

Participatory consciousness
The appeal of animism is that it speaks of the divine in nature.

Owen Barfield, the linguist and friend of C.S. Lewis and J.R.R. Tolkien, calls it 'participatory consciousness'. At first, he argues, people felt they were part of nature.

However, because of the powers of our natural curiosity, we then began to take small steps back from nature, though in the same instant we also perceived that we were different from other animals, for what other animal contemplates its own nature? This is profoundly troubling. No longer were human beings entirely at home. The earliest intimations of existential longing would have emerged: Who are we? Where are we? People sought a new kind of communion with the world, one that is curious about nature, though not alienated from nature, because it still knows it belongs to it. Shamanism and animism are part of that participatory consciousness.

What now? Barfield warns that we cannot simply return to these old forms of consciousness. We know too much, as it were. This is the value of the scientists' contribution.

So what he argues we should seek is a synthesis of the original participation and what he calls final participation. We are passing through a phase of alienation – one that objectifies the world and so brings the understanding of science, but also distances us from nature so that we treat it not as a place to belong but as a resource to exploit by its destruction, even if that destruction may threaten our own future. It is proving unsustainable, and as that fact becomes clearer, an older way of being in the world starts to be important again.

Individuals such as Jane Goodall and David Abram help us to recall our distant original participation. What we need, though, is final participation, a form of consciousness that by deploying the scientific mind in conjunction with a more expansive imagination might move us to a phase where we can know ourselves as of nature and observers of nature. Such a sense is not here yet, on the whole, though various individuals capture glimpses of it, and that draws us not so much back, as forwards.

IS THERE A UNIVERSAL SPIRITUALITY?

Perennial philosophy and a global ethic of realization

The twentieth century was marked by global violence and mass death. Many people's lives were scarred by suffering and loss, and this in turn had a substantial impact upon the way the century thought about religion. One response was a desire to find unity between religions as a counterpoint to the destruction of division.

After the Second World War, a group of scholars formed around what is known as the perennial philosophy, or *philosophia perennis*. In 1945 Aldous Huxley had published a best-selling book by that name, and he offered a definition: the set of beliefs 'that recognizes a divine Reality substantial to the world of things and lives and minds; the psychology that finds in the soul something similar to, or even identical with, divine Reality; the ethic that places man's final end in the knowledge of the immanent and transcendent Ground of all being'.

To put it a little more simply, the broad idea is that underneath the variety of religious systems that have evolved on Earth, there can be discerned a common spirituality. This spirituality is anthropocentric, which is to say that it holds in view the well-being of human individuals and humankind. In some ways, it would make more sense to call the perennial philosophy the 'perennial psychology', as it often draws more on the psychological and spiritual rather than the dogmatic and religious.

A loss of soul

The plausibility of a perennial thesis is readily challenged. Some religions teach a loving relationship with a personal God, whereas others have a sense of depersonalized oneness with the Absolute. Some aspire to transcendence of the physical realm, while others seek an immanence in nature. All major faiths, and many secular systems, teach compassion for other human beings, the so-called golden rule. However, when you ask what compassion involves, differences soon emerge once more. The Judaeo-Christian traditions have taught that divine justice is the necessary corollary of divine love, and so compassion takes the form of mercy. Eastern religions resort to the ancient system of karma, a moral law of cause and effect, from which compassion springs because the compassionate person is the one who sees clearly that everyone is suffering. This is the golden rule as sympathy. The secular version of the golden rule boils down to a different imperative again, essentially an ethic of fairness: each should do or have what others do or have.

Underneath the variety of religious systems that have evolved on Earth, there can be discerned a common spirituality.

That said, there is plenty of evidence that a loose belief in a perennial psychology is appealing to many in the modern world. It springs partly from the feeling that individual spiritual growth matters more than preserving religious institutions, coupled to a sense of crisis about what it is to be human, what it is to flourish, what it is to be whole. So it's worth considering in more depth one version of this gospel. I've picked that of Thomas Moore, a psychotherapist and former monk, who lays it out in his best-selling book *Care of the Soul: How to Add Depth and Meaning to Your Everyday Life*.

Several features are apparent. Moore diagnoses that we live in an age that has suffered a 'loss of soul'. The surface manifestation of this deficit ranges from addictions and obsessions to violence and depression. However, the cause of these symptoms is linked to a deeper crisis of meaning. This can be missed, as the medical approach to such symptoms is to alleviate them, not to try to understand them. This explains why the pharmaceutical industry grows exponentially almost hand in hand with the conditions their pills aim to treat. What we lack, according to Moore, are 'specialists of the soul to advise us when we succumb to moods and emotional pain, or when as a nation we find ourselves confronting a host of threatening evils'.

Carl Jung, a rich resource for perennialists, backs Moore up. Later in his life he observed that the majority of individuals who came to see him, presenting with various mental afflictions, were actually suffering from a crisis of meaning. He proposed, quite plausibly, that the reason psychology had become the dominant source of wisdom in the twentieth century was because the impact that religious systems could make on people's lives had declined. 'Since the stars have fallen from heaven and our highest symbols have paled, a secret life holds sway in the unconscious', he wrote. 'That is why we have a psychology today, and why we speak of the unconscious. All this would be quite superfluous in an age or culture that possessed symbols.'

> *The reason psychology had become the dominant source of wisdom in the twentieth century was because the impact that religious systems could make on people's lives had declined.*

Depth psychology

This raises a second theme that Moore and other perennialists explore: that there are ancient sources of wisdom that we need to recover and renew. That renewal takes place by reinterpreting the old material through the insights of depth psychology, which is the kind of psychology associated with practitioners such as Jung.

What depth psychology allows us to do is pay careful attention to ourselves. Jung envisaged the human person as composed of several layers. There is the conscious layer, of which we are most aware, and with which we can often reason. Beneath that lies an unconscious layer, the highest reaches of which form our personal unconscious. This is the memory of the experiences of our lives and has a profound impact upon us, shown up particularly in our emotional responses to situations, say, of threat or attachment. Then, third, there is a deeper unconscious level that Jung called the collective unconscious. It is the repository of the culture and traditions that form and shape us, and about which we are, typically, unaware. The collective unconscious is like the background or frame through which we experience life. It is the deeper pull that can sometimes be felt in spite of the trivial tugs of the everyday. Falling in love, for example, feels like the most natural thing in the world, though it is simultaneously surprising. It happens to everyone, though to each in a unique way, because love originates in profound urges of the collective unconscious, those that seek unity.

These subterranean layers Jung referred to as the Self, and he believed that the motifs with which the Self is most concerned correspond with common themes in religious traditions. In other words, religion was to our forebears what depth psychology is to us today. Both offer resources for taming and embracing, for nurturing and uncovering the fundamental reality out of which our conscious life springs. We are like plants, Jung suggested. What we consciously notice are the leaves and flowers that sprout and then wither, but that is not the whole of life, for underground lie roots and rhizomes that are the wellsprings of life.

We might refer to the Self, whereas our forebears referred to the world-soul, spirit or God. Hence the link celebrated by the perennial philosophy: the soul as 'something similar to, or even identical with, divine Reality'. Psychology comes close to spirituality in the perennial philosophy, and often, its leading advocates embody a combination of the two disciplines. Moore was a monk and is a psychotherapist. Jung was a psychotherapist and almost a freelance monk, regularly retreating to his private home or cell on the shores of Lake Zurich.

Proportion and harmony

The syncretistic approach is reflected in another of Moore's inspirations, the Renaissance philosopher Marsilio Ficino. Ficino was a 'Renaissance man' in the modern sense too: a master of different branches of knowledge, with the added capacity to knit them together into a coherent whole. He was the head of the Medici academy in fifteenth-century Florence. He almost single-handedly reintroduced the West to the bulk of the works of Plato, when they reappeared from the Muslim world. He wrote broadly on matters from the passions of human love to the esoteric traditions of ancient Egypt. He applied his learning too, notably in *De vita libri tres*, or *Three Books on Life*, a collection of health tips. 'You should walk as often as possible among plants that have a wonderful aroma, spending a considerable amount of time every day among such things', he advises.

Other insights sound less familiar to modern ears. 'I use medicines tempered in accordance with the heavens', he explains, advocating the diagnostic powers of astrology. But whilst the details owe as much to what we would now call magic as science, perennialists are inclined to discern important principles behind the superstition. They believe that it is these principles we have lost sight of today.

Music provides an interesting case in point. Ficino reflects extensively on the spiritual power of music. 'I often resort to the solemn sound of the lyre and to singing to raise the mind to the highest considerations and to God as much as I may.' He noted that ancient shrines to Apollo were not just places of music and spirituality, but music and healing. The strings of Orpheus' lyre he likens to a model for harmony in

ORPHEUS, FROM THE SERIES 'THE PROGRESS OF HUMAN CULTURE AND KNOWLEDGE' (C. 1777–84) BY JAMES BARRY. ANCIENT MUSIC WAS THOUGHT TO HAVE HEALING PROPERTIES, A NOTION CAPTURED IN THE MYTHS SURROUNDING ORPHEUS, WHO IS ALWAYS DEPICTED WITH A LYRE.

161

the cosmos. 'By the sounding strings, that is, by their vibrations and power', he regulates everything; by the lowest string, winter; by the highest string, summer; and by the middle strings, he brings in spring and autumn.' This is an image of proportion and harmony, one that works on the body via the senses and on the soul via a notion of spiritual assent. The upshot is that music has a healing effect, because when we hear it, we feel its subtle combinations of consonance and dissonance, of stillness and flow, of law and freedom. In an embodied manner, it teaches us how spiritually to live.

> *Music has a healing effect, because when we hear it, we feel its subtle combinations of consonance and dissonance, of stillness and flow, of law and freedom.*

Today, Western music has two dominant modes, major and minor. Very, very roughly speaking, one is bright and uplifting, the other melancholic and expressive. However, in Ficino's day, musicians worked in seven modes. The Dorian, Phrygian, Lydian, Mixolydian and Locrian offer subtle variations in mood from the Aeolian and Ionian that correspond to major and minor as we know them. Ever since Pythagoras, musicologists had been interested in the mathematical ratios that underpin each mode. But they were also interested in why human beings find some modes pleasant, others troubling; some mysterious, others tranquil. Somehow or other, music speaks to the soul. Hence its healing and spiritual power.

It is this holism that appeals to perennialists today, what Moore calls 'poetic holding'. Responding to a person as a living soul might lead 'more deeply into the body and its pain than do measurements and univocal, purely physical interpretations'. Moore is a both/and person rather than an either/or: the medicine of music is complementary, in the strict sense that it might complete what conventional medicine overlooks. 'Clarity is not one of the gifts of poetry', he continues. 'On the other hand, poetry does provide depth, insight, wisdom, vision, language, and music. We simply don't think about these qualities much when faced with illness.'

Perhaps not much, but possibly more than we used to.
There is also a growing recognition that modern music is, in some
respects, a narrower phenomenon than it was in Renaissance
Europe. The commercial success of recordings of monks intoning
ancient chants in the older modes is one indicator of that.
Electronic chill-out music often flirts with the various scales too.
And music therapies are becoming more mainstream.

In a recent article in *The Lancet*, the professor of medical
humanities Martyn Evans commented that 'The relevance of
[music] to health and illness might not immediately be apparent
but both the fact of music's enormous hold on us, and the kind
of explanation we might give for it, are important for clinical
medicine.' He advocated asking why music has therapeutic effects,
rather than how – the kind of question that seeks mechanical
explanations and so may be distracting. His answer resonates well
with that of Ficino, for all that he makes no references to Orpheus
or the stars. That would grate in a leading medical journal.

'When music works upon us therapeutically, it expresses,
recalls, and even rekindles general features of our embodied
experience and of our ordinary being', Evans writes. This is not
a mechanical process, but one that 'inclines us in the direction
of bodily and psychological fluency and vitality'. Further, he
speculates, music may be 'an expression not merely of our
ordinary being but of our place in the universal order of things.
Were this so, it would invite a far more radical conception of why
music can always console us and, sometimes, can heal us.'

It is such radical conceptions of what it is to be human that a
perennial psychology encourages us to consider. It is experimental,
eclectic, even excessive. But there is a reason it finds a following. It
attends to the soul in a world suffering from a loss of soul.

Macro and micro

Stepping back from the specifics of music, there is another general
principle that perennialism makes much of: the microcosm as
a reflection of the macrocosm. The ordinary, humdrum world

around us replicates perfect and divine realities. It is rather like
a fractal pattern: as you zoom in and pan out, the bud-like
configurations stay the same, regardless of scale.

It is for this reason that people were very interested in
astrology. It was not, at its best, like the tabloid discipline of today,
where a newspaper astrologer files portraits of what a Sagittarian or
Libran can expect to happen tomorrow. Instead, the main idea was
that earthly forces are matched in the heavens. Hence, whilst it
is often very difficult to see clearly what is happening on Earth, it is
possible to chart the precise and predictable movement of celestial
bodies. What is above can, therefore, be used to interpret the
confusing complexities of life below.

Astrology died as a serious science when the Aristotelian
cosmology upon which it is based was usurped by the Copernican:
we are not at the centre of things any more, at least in a
straightforwardly astronomical sense. However, the notion that the
micro and the macro are related has other manifestations.

The idea is central to much Platonic thought. A physicist,
for example, can write an equation upon the blackboard and report
to his attentive students that it describes precisely what will happen
to a cluster of galaxies many thousands of light years away. That is a
remarkable link between the near and far, above and below.

Alternatively, activities as apparently dissimilar as the global
fashion industry and the work of the United Nations can be
interpreted in similar ways. The fashion industry is a kind of huge
game in which people play at beauty. But it is a game fashionistas in
Milan can join with the stylish in Tokyo; the hemlines sewn in New
York make sense to individuals in Beijing. It raises the possibility that
behind the multiple forms of beauty being paraded along the catwalk
lies a singular form of beauty that, whilst never wholly realized, is
perpetually being chased. The particular faintly mirrors the universal.

The work of the United Nations could be said to deploy
this Platonic perennialism at the level of morals. What are universal

human rights if not truths that hold always and everywhere? If one person suffers, we all suffer, runs the human rights motto. Freedom, justice and equality mean infinitely various things to different people, and yet they can be enshrined in a common, international law. You can think global and local.

An imaginary spiritual life

It might be said that we are all perennialists now. The philosophy fits a world culture. That must be another reason why it resonates with so many. The difference is that the preferred mode of expression of an explicit perennial philosophy is not mathematics, or fashion, or rights, but spirit. The poet Thomas Traherne caught the theme in this mode when he reflected upon the nature of the atom. The smallest detail of the world is a divine disclosure, he discerned. All partake of the One:

> *When in all its operations I behold an atom and see it representing my God unto me: when I behold a mirror of his essence in it and a temple of his presence, a token of his love, and an offspring of his will, an attendant upon his throne, an object of his joy, a spectacle of his eye, a work of his hand, a subject of his pleasure, and a means of his glory!*

All that from one atom.

Such a sensibility can be criticized as sheer fantasy, of course. More substantially, the Platonism that underlines perennialism is heavily critiqued in philosophy. In fact, it was first critiqued by Plato himself: he has yet to be beaten at discerning the flaws in his own ideas. We saw a reflection of that in the opening comments to this big question, which noted that the golden rule, say, is actually pretty diverse. But there is one criticism that it is worth remembering especially if you incline to the spiritual universalism of the perennial philosophy.

There is a danger that this approach will abstract you from the world. If your attention is drawn to the Good rather than what is good, to Beauty rather than the beautiful, to the galaxies not Earth, you may lose interest in this life and long for another. The

> *People go to a church or mosque or temple not to remove themselves from the world but in order to engage more deeply in it.*

transcendent whole appeals more than the immanent particular. It's far easier to live in the clouds. And so perennialism may become a world-denying, possibly world-loathing philosophy.

You sense this sometimes if you meet individuals who are heavily influenced by it, regarding it as the truly enlightened state. Their smiles are perfectly formed but somehow their eyes are empty. They are so heavenly minded that they are no earthly good. It thins their humanity rather than amplifying it.

What has happened, in Moore's terms, is that the person is attempting to live an imaginary spiritual life, and mistaking that for using their spiritual imagination to enliven this life. It is to safeguard against this risk that all authentic forms of spirituality emphasis that the real is found amidst the mundane, not elsewhere. The world of the divine is embedded in the world of things. Sincere faith is married to good works. Moore stresses the 'soul's need for vernacular life – its relationship to a local place and culture'. He continues: 'It has a preference for details and particulars, intimacy and involvement, attachment and rootedness . . . To the soul, the ordinary is sacred and the everyday is the primary source of religion.'

People go to a church or mosque or temple not to remove themselves from the world but in order to engage more deeply in it. Retreats and pilgrimages are exceptional times because they reinvigorate a consciousness of how to perceive spiritual values in the ordinary.

To state the obvious, we must each live a particular life. It is bound to a specific time, form and culture. If the perennial philosophy seduces you into thinking you can live on a higher plane, it may be encouraging you not to live at all.

DOES HUMAN SUFFERING RULE OUT GOD?

The problem of evil and the humanity of hope

O ne of the times I felt close to evil was in Cambodia. I had been visiting Angkor Wat, the best-known and most spectacular of the temples that surround Siem Reap, built between the ninth and eleventh centuries by the Khmer kings. In terms of scale, they outdo the grandest cathedrals of medieval Europe. But our guide wanted to show us other sites too, ones that spoke more of poignancy than grandiosity.

The particular temple he had in mind was called Banteay Samré. It is not as impressive as Angkor War or others like the Bayon, famous for the serene smiling faces of the Buddha of compassion that stand in relief from the stone of its towers. Banteay Samré is a little off the beaten track.

The temples are symbolic representations of the cosmos, with the central towers depicting Mount Meru, the navel of the universe in Hindu mythology. The ornate central piles are surrounded by shrines and rectangular galleries; Banteay Samré has two such cloisters, one inside the other. But if the temples exemplify what a civilization can achieve at its peak, this temple was also the site of humanity at its most depraved.

In the late 1970s the Khmer Rouge turned Banteay Samré into a penal complex. The holy galleries were divided into airless cells. Out of a temple was fashioned a hell hole: the day we visited, it was 40 degrees in the shade. People were bricked into this prison and forgotten. Before the monument could be reopened to the public, mounds of human bones had to be cleared from its enclosures and cells.

Like most Cambodians now approaching middle age, our guide at Banteay Samré lives with his own memories of the regime. His parents had been teachers; just before Pol Pot began his experiment in agrarian communism, they were savvy enough to leave the university and school where they had taught and take up life as farmers. When the henchmen came to call, they had calluses on their hands and so could 'prove' they were not intellectuals.

He himself was separated from his parents and moved to a commune of about a thousand children. During the next few years, his four sisters died, along with many hundreds of others. Famine was the biggest killer, along with hideous punishments.

One day, driven by hunger, he and three other boys stole some potatoes. The other three were caught and shot, their bodies tossed into a ditch. Our guide escaped only because, on impulse, he came back by a different route. Another day, one of the men in charge of the children asked the commune commander whether rations might be increased, since so many were dying. The commander decided to make an example of the man. He ordered someone to cut down a dead palm branch, the edges of which are as strong and sharp as a notched steel saw. As the children watched, the man had his head cut off, by degrees. Each time he passed out, he was revived with water.

Angkor Wat itself carries scars from the time too, including shrapnel marks on the walls. And our guide pointed us to another grizzly detail. One of the gallery walls depicts the mythological levels of hell in detailed bas-reliefs. As you descend, the tortures become more brutal. Close to the abyss are images of victims being tied to frames with nails driven into their arms and legs. The Khmer Rouge stole the idea and made the mythological actual. In real life, there was a nail in the body for every question someone couldn't or wouldn't answer.

The killing fields have now been replanted, and corruption seems to be the biggest problem facing Cambodians today. But won't this evil be addressed? we asked. Will there be a truth and reconciliation commission, we wondered, seeking signs of hope? After all, many of those who committed crimes must still live in the country.

Our guide smiled. Most people want to put these things to the back of their minds, he explained. He argued that justice was not really possible because of the scale of what had happened: you'd have to haul a significant percentage of the population into the courts, and society would be destroyed in the process. People prefer to forget – only they don't, of course. And maybe something else is possible.

Dualism of good and evil

What that might be struck me recently, when a journalist tracked down one Khmer prison chief and reflected that what he found was not just a criminal, but more profoundly, understanding. The great lesson, Nic Dunlop explained, is that at the end of a trail of torture and suffering, you find a wizened old man who appears to be contrite about his role in some of the worst crimes of the twentieth century. 'As long as he remains a human being, and that's what I found, there is hope', said Dunlop.

When there is no practical justice that can deal with what has happened, it is as if an alternative imperative comes through. Can we view such atrocities in a place beyond good and evil, as it were, and in that way comprehend the horror a little, punish in small part those responsible – but mostly live on with hope in spite of the past?

Hope can find a place alongside the hurt and damage when individuals caught up in the events manage to commit to life once more.

169

What I heard the journalist saying was that hope can find a place alongside the hurt and damage when individuals caught up in the events manage to commit to life once more.

I think that this is what religious approaches to the reality of evil try to offer. It is rather different from the way the existence of suffering is treated, in the philosophy of religion, as a logical problem. How can a good God sanction or allow such suffering? It is a major issue, probably the most persuasive reason for not believing in God. It gets you in the gut. And that's the problem with the philosophical debate: it does not.

The arguments tend to go something like this. If God is the best explanation for a good world, then how come that same God allows the existence of death and pain? Isn't it more sensible to assume that good and evil have the same status: neither needs God? From this it is a small step to concluding that there is no God. That solves the embarrassing paradox of the believer who would praise an omnipotent, all-good God from whom all blessings flow, but who does not curse that same God from whom all evils must flow too.

In fact, some theologies do attribute good and evil both to God. Gnostic doctrines tend to do so. The Manichaeans of the early Christian centuries, for example, taught that the material world is caught up in an archetypal conflict between good and evil. Good is represented by the light, evil by darkness. The conflict is not only fought in the external world, but internally inside each of us. We have two wills: one good, one evil. Our psychological struggles are manifestations of this moral tug of war. The aim of religion is to release the light from the powers of darkness, something that can only finally be achieved outside of the material realm.

This dualism of good and evil is a plausible theology that has been reinvented, with variations, throughout history. Whenever Satan or some kind of supreme devil is invoked as the source of all evil, that is a sign of this approach.

One of the great reinterpretations of the twentieth century is found in the writings of Carl Jung. He argued that each of us possesses a shadow, a dark side to our character that threatens to overwhelm us at any moment. It explains why usually decent people commit terrible crimes of passion, or why whole societies can be consumed by violent convulsions such as the world wars that occurred during Jung's lifetime. The way to deal with this evil presence, at least on an individual level, is to reconcile the shadow with the good in us, a process Jung called individuation. It requires the courage to face evil, something that Jung thought theistic religions, worshipping a good God, find impossible to do.

The nature of evil

The traditional Christian response to the presence of evil is to argue that it is not anything substantial in itself. Rather, it is the absence of good. The idea is popularly captured in Edmund Burke's comment: 'It is necessary only for the good man to do nothing for evil to triumph.' Nothing, as it were, does the work of evil.

Augustine formulated the full doctrine, defining evil in the negative as the privation of goodness (*privatio boni*). He drew on Plotinus, who used the analogy of disease to explain evil:

> *The traditional Christian response to the presence of evil is to argue that it is not anything substantial in itself. Rather, it is the absence of good.*

> *For what is that which we call evil but the absence of good? In the bodies of animals, disease and wounds mean nothing but the absence of health; for when a cure is affected, that does not mean that the evils which were present – namely, the disease and wounds – go away from the body and dwell elsewhere; they altogether cease to exist.*

It gets God out of the dock because God has done nothing for evil to exist. Evil is a kind of misapprehension, as Mary Baker Eddy instructed the followers of Christian Science: 'all inharmony of mortal mind or body is illusion, possessing neither reality nor identity though seeming to be real and identical'. However, it is wholly inadequate to call evil an illusion. The killing fields of the world seem pretty real to most people. And it provokes the retort that if God sustains everything that exists, then surely He sustains evil too, even if He is not responsible for its genesis.

In fact, the Christian doctrine is more subtle. Evil is not literally nothing. It is rather the absence of something that should be present, namely God's goodness. The problem of evil is, therefore, reframed as the problem of a lack of goodness.

This comes in two forms. Sometimes the lack of goodness can be put down to natural suffering. This in turn can be understood as the fact that what is good for one creature may well be bad for another. The theologian Herbert McCabe explains:

> *When I suffer from a disease it is because the bacteria or whatever are fulfilling themselves and behaving exactly as good bacteria should behave. If we found a bacterium which was not engaged in inflicting disease on me we should have to judge that, like a washing machine that did not wash clothes, it was a defective or sick bacterium.*

Natural evil is the by-product of another natural good. One follows the other. The lion kills the gazelle so that her cubs may eat and live. Earthquakes are caused by plate tectonics, which is a good in so far as it also recycles the minerals of the Earth's crust. Pain is a consequence of the good offered by the body's instant warning system that it is in danger. If a believer falls ill then they will, of course, go to the doctor and hope for a cure. However, the faithful response to the question *why me?* is really *why not me?* Such suffering is part of what it is to live – that overarching good that God wants and wills.

However, there is another kind of evil, known as moral evil. Here, evil does have a cause: not God, but the wickedness of human beings. The killing fields are a brutal example.

Now, it might be argued that God keeps wicked human beings in existence and so is responsible for moral evil too. However, wickedness is not like the blind evil of natural suffering. It is willed. Torturers and tyrants delight in the exercise of their powers. God is, therefore, only indirectly responsible for these ills, it is argued. The primary responsibility rests with the evil-doers themselves. God allows them to commit their crimes, but that is only because He allows all human beings to be responsible for their acts – good ones too. We are not puppets, we are people.

> *God allows them to commit their crimes, but that is only because He allows all human beings to be responsible for their acts – good ones too.*

There are all kinds of objections to the *privatio boni* account of evil. One is that it seems relatively easy to imagine a world in which there is more good than this one, and so less evil. Is this then the best of all possible worlds? Theologians have argued that only God could answer such a question, and that must, in principle, be right: what kind of calculation could we perform to decide the issue, given our limited view? If you say you could design a world without earthquakes, then how would you recycle minerals? If you say you would intervene when a wicked person was about to act, then why not intervene when someone was about to do something stupid, or just not very sensible? Where would you draw the line? You would turn human beings into puppets.

But anyway, these kind of debates seem to miss the emotional force behind the objection. What is really disagreeable about declaring that this must be the best of all possible worlds is the complacency it implies. What about the evil, the suffering, the injustice, the horror? How can one hold on to hope in the face of it? Well, this is, I suspect, what less philosophical, more religious approaches to the reality of evil strive to sustain.

Suffering and humanity

There is a very different approach in the literature and iconography of the great spiritual traditions. In the Hebrew Bible,

CHRIST ON THE CROSS, DETAIL FROM THE ISENHEIM ALTARPIECE (c. 1512–15) BY MATTHIAS GRÜNEWALD. ONE OF THE MOST VIVID PICTURES OF CHRIST SUFFERING THAT CAN BE TAKEN AS INSPIRING DEEP FEELINGS OF HUMAN SYMPATHY IN THE VIEWER.

the book of Job is key. The life of this innocent man is ruined by terrible afflictions, sanctioned by God, though performed by Satan. His three friends act as philosopher and suggest reasons why he has suffered so. None of them stand up. Then, at the end, God himself appears to Job. It leaves Job speechless. He realizes that he understands very little about the divine will and the ways of the world. He is not even privy to what the reader knows about God's earlier conversations with Satan.

In an epilogue, God condemns the philosopher friends for not appreciating their ignorance. They must ask forgiveness of Job. As for Job, he is restored to his former wealth and happiness, though the reader is left wondering about the loved ones he had previously lost.

The story has provoked endless debate, not least on whether God is a tyrant who pulls rank on suffering creatures. But that, in a sense, is the remarkable issue. This is a book of the Bible. It powerfully contemplates that possibility. It can't be an argument in defence of God. There are too many obvious holes to pick. Instead, the book must function as a catharsis for believers. It is like the psalms and the wisdom literature, also contained in the scriptures. The assumption is that evil exists. That much is clear. The biblical approach is not to deny the undeniable, to explain the inexplicable. It is to try to stare it in the face.

This attitude accounts for what is otherwise an oddity: that the greatest religious innovators were individuals who were fully acquainted with evil too. Think of the Buddha, who is said to have heard his religious calling when he became aware of the suffering of the world. He sought a way of dealing with suffering, not by denying its existence, but by transforming the individual's

The biblical approach is not to deny the undeniable, to explain the inexplicable. It is to try to stare it in the face.

perception of it. It is no more, or less, than the constant play of cause and effect. 'By oneself, indeed, is evil done; by oneself is one defiled', notes the *Dhammapada*. All deeds have consequences, some bad, some good. They are played out in the cycle of rebirths. The Buddha's way is not to end suffering but to find release within it.

The medieval Christian tradition is arguably quite similar. After the turn of the first millennium, there was an explosion of devotional imagery depicting the passion of Christ – assorted scenes of the mocking, crucifixion, death and deposition of Jesus – clearly intended to provoke compassion in those who gazed on them. Again, suffering is not being negated. It is being seen for what it is. It is being contemplated in the figure of Christ, for the believer who can bear to look. As Ludolph of Saxony, a Carthusian monk of the fourteenth century, wrote:

> *It is sweeter to view you as dying before the Jews on the tree than as holding sway over the angels in Heaven; to see you as a man bearing every aspect of human nature to the end than as God manifesting divine nature; to see you as the dying Redeemer than as the invisible Creator.*

The humanity is what counts, as Nic Dunlop discovered. For with humanity comes dignity, the quality that emerges from the brave souls who have seen and suffered great evil. If I came about as close as I ever have done to great evil in Cambodia, I felt too that I'd come about as close as I ever would to a 'solution' to the problem of evil. Our guide told his story calmly, compassionately. He knew evil. He still knew hope.

CAN WE BE GOOD WITHOUT GOD?

Atheists are good, believers bad, but there's more to say

You don't need to believe in God to be good, or at least you don't need to believe in God to hope to be good. As clearly as the day is light, there have lived highly principled individuals who didn't set any store by faith. Some have no doubt thought themselves principled because they were not religious.

Conscientiousness is desirable and admirable not because any divinity tells you to be so but because you tell yourself to be so. There are other non-religious foundations of morality, human foundations. It might be the feeling of human sympathy, the recognition that I am because you are and so others' needs and aspirations carry a validity equal to my own. It might be the feeling of human will, the recognition that if there is no external authority to guide our actions, then we must cultivate and assert our own self-responsible authority.

And anyway, aren't the vast majority of people reasonable, once the heat of anger, revenge or jealousy has died down? Most folk are sincere folk. They are prepared to follow the so-called harm principle of John Stuart Mill: that you can do what you like so long as you don't hurt others. They understand that if my desire to wear a mink on my shoulders, or cheap shoes upon my feet, causes great suffering in the lives of other sentient beings, then it is only right that I adjust my preferences and so ease the general suffering. Common sense and common decency will carry you a long way along the path of moral considerations, and when decisions become more complex and difficult, the demands of justice, responsibility and empathy will do much of the rest.

Why be good without God? Because we can. God might be a fiction some choose to deploy when encouraging themselves or others to behave well, but it is really a childish ploy, similar to the parent who bribes their child with a promise of jam tomorrow.

Broadly speaking, something like this is the view that secular philosophers have of what it takes to be moral. If you read a great writer in the field, such as David Hume, it is everyday moral sentiments such as concern and conviviality that he builds on. If you read someone who follows Immanuel Kant, they will attempt to persuade you that lying is wrong by way of moral reasoning: if you lie to others then how can you expect them not to lie to you? Again, it is a thoroughly this-worldly, practical morality. Many religious moralists today follow suit. The former Bishop of Edinburgh, Richard Holloway, wrote a book called *Godless Morality*. He noted that while it may be the case that there is 'a connection between religious decline and ethical confusion, and most observers would probably accept that there is', there is no point in addressing moral concerns by trying to revivify religion. For good, then, we need a non-religious morality. And this should be possible. After all, is it more important to believe that wife-beaters go to hell or that a man should stop beating his wife? Clearly the latter, which proves that there is at least one moral conviction that can be affirmed without believing in hell, or God.

> *Why be good without God? Because we can.*

So why does this big question never quite go away? What do religious believers fear is lost when the link between goodness and godliness is severed? Could it even be that secular moral philosophers secretly worry that more is at risk too?

Losing touch with reality

One immediate concern is captured by the Christian doctrine of original sin. It was well summarized by St Paul, when he observed

177

ADAM AND EVE (1504) BY ALBRECHT DÜRER. THE TRAGEDY OF THE HUMAN CONDITION, EXPRESSED IN ORIGINAL SIN, IS CAPTURED IN THE MYTH OF ADAM AND EVE EXPELLED FROM THE GARDEN OF EDEN.

that frequently he does things he tries not to do, and doesn't do things he wishes he would and knows he ought to do.

This represents a pessimistic though not unrealistic view of human nature, one held in common with the ancient Greek notion of tragedy – that good individuals inevitably do bad things and as a result innocents and innocence suffers. It is also similar to the modern Freudian notion in psychoanalysis. Freud's 'original sin' stems not from the temptation of Adam and Eve, but from the complications of childhood. He argues that every child experiences aggressive emotions directed at its parents because while the child depends upon them, it is driven by the urge to be independent of them too. That is only to grow up. The difficulty is that the aggression conflicts with the love the child feels for its parents, and so the aggression, out of shame, goes underground, building up in the child's unconscious, like the pressure behind a head of steam, until it is released, leading to the formation of the superego. The superego is the voice of conscience, an internal judge, an impartial spectator. It turns the built-up aggression against the child itself, manifest in overwhelming feelings of guilt. The saint, then, has it right: although everyone tells them that they are an admirable person, they know they are still a sinner. They feel it inside. They carry an original conflict within themselves that will never allow them to be simply, straightforwardly good.

It can seem an overly dramatic account of human behaviour, and one without hope. But at least it recognizes the panoply of ills that pervade the human world. If people were self-consciously greedy, selfish, exploitative, unjust, hateful, sadistic and violent, that would be bad enough, though being self-consciously so might hold out the hope that it is possible to correct such behaviour. But it seems pretty conclusive that people are *involuntarily* rapacious, egotistical, unfair, abusive, loathing, cruel and vicious too. Righting these wrongs requires a solution of an altogether different order, because we often do not know what we are doing, as Paul observed of himself. Individuals cannot fix themselves, the doctrine of original sin says. We cannot simply will ourselves not to harm others. Along with Freud and the ancient Greeks, the pessimistic/realistic view of human nature counsels that the individual needs to die to themselves in order to be redeemed.

The hero in the ancient Greek tragedy sacrifices himself, and in the act of dying is recognized as praiseworthy by the gods. In Freudian analysis, the individual achieves a degree of recognition of their inner state, and realizes that the pathway to change is via the painful giving up of comforting delusions. In Christianity, Jesus demonstrates that the only way out of the nexus created by sin is death. 'The coming of the kingdom', Terry Eagleton explains in *Reason, Faith, and Revolution,*

> *involves not a change of government, but a turbulent passage through death, nothingness, madness, loss, and futility … There is no possibility of a smooth evolution here. Given the twisted state of the world, self-fulfillment can ultimately come about only through self-divestment.*

Jesus said that only the person who loses their life will save it, a diagnosis that can be found in other religions too. So the first element that the religious believer worries is lost in the insistence that you can be good without God is a clear view of the harshness of reality. The problem with losing touch with the reality of the foul play that Christians call sin is that it leaves you deluded, as if human sympathy or sheer will could put matters right. In fact delusion, deepened by its denials, is likely to make matters worse, since we are not facing up to the situation as it actually is. 'It is surely in the tissue of that life that the secrets of good and evil are to be found', wrote Iris Murdoch, in her essay 'On "God" and "Good"'. She continues: 'What we really are seems much more like an obscure system of energy out of which choices and visible acts of will emerge at intervals in ways which are often unclear.'

A second aspect that is feared lost is a certain kind of objectivity in ethics. By this, I don't primarily mean an ability to assert that something is absolutely right or wrong, always and everywhere, on the grounds that God has decreed it so. This is known as divine command theory: the notion that something is right because God says it is right, and wrong because God rules that too. The trouble for religious folk who like their ethics served so simple is that even in divine command theory, the individual believer is urged to deploy their reason in order to work out what God has decreed, for the obvious reason that beyond a handful of useful commandments, it is typically far from clear what God might bless or forbid on a day-by-day basis. Further, the richest accounts of divine command theory insist that the interpretation of written scriptures and oral traditions is a necessary part of ascertaining God's law. It is not an optional extra but an integral part of the discovery, as only through that struggle can the believer truly align their will with God's.

I also don't think it is true that only religious people can believe that some imperatives are absolutely and always true, aside from the interpretative task. The utilitarian ethicist Peter Singer, for example, is an atheist, though he has recently come around to believing that some ethical truths are objective truths. He had followed the fashion amongst moral philosophers, which took a lead from Hume. Hume had concluded that the reasons human beings offer to justify their actions will always contain, if not conceal, the desires that led the individual to perform those actions. I may say that I visit my crotchety uncle in the nursing home out of duty and love, when really I visit him to appease the guilt I feel for putting him there in the first place. Ethical decisions always contain an element of such self-justificatory rationalization, Hume suspected – feelings disguised as reasons. But if that is so, it is also the case that feelings and desires cannot be right or wrong; they are simply feelings and desires. So if they are intimately caught up in our moral assertions, there can be no absolutely right or wrong judgements about our actions either.

Singer once agreed with this, though he has now changed his mind. He has concluded that there are some things we deem right or wrong not out of any process of dodgy reasoning, but because we intuit them to be so. An example might be that inflicting needless suffering is always bad.

> *The reasons human beings offer to justify their actions will always contain, if not conceal, the desires that led the individual to perform those actions.*

A wider horizon

The objective aspect of goodness that I want to focus on is about something else. It is not about what we do, but where we are going. It is not about our feelings in life, but our view of life beyond our own immediate concerns. This is the other sense in which morality can be objective: being about more than just our subjective feelings or rationalizations. What is good stands over us, as it were, though not only to judge us, but to draw us too, with its beauty.

It draws us because it promises our flourishing alongside the flourishing of all else besides. The ethical life in this objective sense seeks a broader view than just what concerns the individual and his or her actions moment by moment. The seeker after the good life does pay attention to his or her will and choices, but they also have an eye for a wider horizon, a horizon that would persist even if there were not humans seeking it out. This is what believers call God, and why many still insist godliness is intimately connected to goodness, even if the godliness is not acknowledged.

Iris Murdoch associates the loss of such a concept of goodness in contemporary moral life with the dominance of the language of moral rights. If goodness needs a moral background, a view of life that reaches beyond the concerns of the individual to a perception of what is good regardless of what we think, rights do not. They can be focused more narrowly on human worth and activity alone. The moral life is conceived of solely as a matter of personal responsibility and sincerity. 'The agent, thin as a needle, appears in the quick flash of the choosing will', writes Murdoch. There is nothing wrong with that per se. Clearly, human worth, responsibility and sincerity are goods and virtues, not vices. The issue, though, is whether they are enough – which is to point back to the problem of original sin.

If that conception of the human condition is accepted, there is a further problem for the godless. How might they glimpse that broader horizon, particularly given the delusions that cloud our view, which are part of sin too?

Murdoch reflects on the religious practice of prayer. She suggests that it is not best thought of as a form of petition, as if prayer is about asking God for this or that, but rather as a form of attention. Focusing the attention on a goodness that is beyond immediate desires and needs is very different from envisaging the moral life as one of right judgement or correct choices. 'The religious believer, especially if his God is conceived of as a person, is in the fortunate position of being able to focus his thought upon something which is a source of energy', Murdoch continues. This source of goodness does not attempt to struggle against the forces of selfishness and aggression in the individual. Instead, it might feed the individual with a different kind of vigour, refocusing them rather than attempting to reprogramme them. Instead of being attached to that which morally trips us up, we might in time become attached to that which morally lifts us up.

> *Instead of being attached to that which morally trips us up, we might in time become attached to that which morally lifts us up.*

An analogy can be found with art. The artist does not paint something so as to tell you that they like that bowl of fruit or those rolling hills. They paint it for the object's own sake. The best artists are not self-aggrandizing but other-attending. They do not seek to indulge their fantasies but almost impersonally to glimpse reality. They disappear in their art, as Virginia Woolf observed in the case of William Shakespeare. We know so little of him, she mused in *A Room of One's Own*, because he lost his interest in himself. He died to himself and so could live for his art:

> *All desire to protest, to preach, to proclaim an injury, to pay off a score, to make the world the witness of some hardship or grievance was fired out of him and consumed. Therefore his poetry flows from him free and unimpeded.*

Murdoch adds: 'The greatest art is "impersonal" because it shows us the world, our world and not another one, with a clarity which startles and delights us simply because we are not used to looking at the real world at all.'

The absence of transcendent goodness

This reference to art raises the possibility that the object of moral attention need not in fact be God. Murdoch affirms that too, noting how philosophers in this tradition of morality have long argued that focusing the attention on all manner of objects that are valuable might have similar effects. It might be great people, the heroes that an individual desires to emulate. This is what the heroic tradition of ancient Greece commends. It might be great art, the representations that subtly shape our inner images of what is good. Religion encourages devotion to non-divine objects too, in the lives of the saints or the music and symbolism that surround worship. As the writer of the letter to the Philippians has it:

> *Whatsoever things are true, whatsoever things are honest, whatsoever things are just, whatsoever things are pure, whatsoever things are lovely, whatsoever things are of good report; if there be any virtue, if there be any praise, think on these things.*

That said, learning to love the good people or things that might shift egocentric preoccupations and struggles is more than just a form of neurolinguistic reprogramming. The problem with reducing this approach to the deployment of a 'psychological device', as Iris Murdoch puts it, is that it loses touch with the specifically objective view of morality we have been considering. It is not an objectivity that seeks moral certainty, but one that seeks a wider horizon to walk towards. If prayer and sustained attention is merely a method for tricking the flawed mind, the authority for deciding what should be contemplated – what is worthy of attention – remains in the realm of the human and subjective. Who decides what is good: a parent, a politician, a philosopher, a critic? Their horizons will be their own. They will be implicated in the moral malaise of original sin too.

I imagine that this is why Jesus is remembered for commanding, 'Be ye perfect.' If he had advised, 'Be ye a bit better', he would have invited his disciples to engage in a process of comparing and contrasting their behaviour. Uneasy competition would have ruled amongst them, rather than loving striving after perfection. As we who live in a world that is ruled by the institutions of free markets can see very clearly, competition is a formula that can improve goods and services, but it must also pay the price of greed, selfishness, exploitation, injustice and violence. It does not make for a good world. It makes for a good and bad world.

Hence, in her essay Iris Murdoch stresses that a conception of the transcendent is necessary. The origin or source of moral goodness needs ultimately to rest beyond human flaws, for all that it will always be mediated to us through flawed means because we are human.

The sceptic about transcendent goodness and/or God will find this troubling. They will suspect that a longing after transcendence is really a longing after the consolation of there being moral purpose in the blind cosmos after all. It's a dream

> *The origin or source of moral goodness needs ultimately to rest beyond human flaws, for all that it will always be mediated to us through flawed means because we are human.*

that, far from being real, is the deepest fantasy, they might maintain. Of course. There is no quick argument to settle the case, and anyway, the argument here is that an activity other than reason must be allowed a space too. At the end of the day it is not philosophy that can convince anyone. It is a loving attention and disciplined detachment akin to that demonstrated by the artist who dies to themselves for the sake of their art; what religious traditions call meditation or prayer.

The elements that may be lost with the absence of a transcendent source of goodness are then, broadly, twofold. First is an account of human nature that is realistic, seemingly bleak, but prepared to recognize that human sympathy and will fall short when we are at war with ourselves and others. Transformation not amelioration is our fundamental moral need.

Second is a sense of our moral task that includes the search for a transcendent horizon, not because it delivers moral certainties, but because it fires high, impossible moral aspirations. It is like the magnetic force field felt by what is sometimes referred to as our 'moral compass', the energy known in experiences of virtue, beauty and love that orientates us aright, if only momentarily.

If either of these losses concerns you, then you may also be inclined to believe that if it is not impossible to be good without God, it is harder.

ARE WE LIVING IN THE END TIMES?
Global catastrophe, moral rage, and the thrill of the Rapture

*I*n 2011 former engineer and radio preacher Harold Camping became global news when he set a date for the end of the world: 21 May 2011. Camping had a long interest in biblical numerology, scouring the books of Daniel and Revelation for hidden clues that spoke of the Rapture, and he spent significant amounts of money promoting his prophecy. But it was remarkable that so many news outlets channelled it, flashing it to the four corners of the planet. Why? What was the appeal of a story that was dismissed in almost the same breath it was reported in?

In truth, the end times is a trope that has wide appeal, far beyond the dark corners of esoteric religion. The novelist A.S. Byatt, who asserts that 'religion has gone away', for herself at least, nonetheless devoted her considerable literary talents to a rewriting of the ancient Norse myths of apocalypse, in her book *Ragnarok: The End of the Gods*.

It is a particularly bleak tradition. In Christianity and Islam, God brings about the end of the world, but apocalypse is also a time of redemption, when what is good is saved. In the Norse myths, even the gods are destroyed. They tell of an apocalypse to end apocalypses. 'The wolf swallowed the king of the gods, the snake poisoned Thor, everything was burned in a red light and drowned in blackness', Byatt writes. Such utter calamity reflects what she felt as a child, growing up during the Second World War, and also what she feels about the world now, facing daily ecological destruction. In an essay on the book, published in the *Guardian* newspaper, she explained,

> *Every day I read of a new extinction, of the bleaching of the coral and the disappearance of the codfish … I read of human projects that destroy the world they are in, ingeniously, ambitiously engineered oil wells in deep water, a road across the migration paths of the beasts in the Serengeti park, farming of asparagus in Peru… Almost all the scientists I know think we are bringing about our own extinction, more and more rapidly.*

Secular apocalyptic myths can be painted as events that are powerfully realistic too. It is common in sci-fi. Such a strategy is adopted in Steve Aylett's short story 'Gigantic', collected in *The Apocalypse Reader*, edited by Justin Taylor. Aylett begins by describing a sudden appearance over the White House: a screaming sound accompanies the opening of an eye-like aperture in an airship floating above it. Similar doors are creaking into action all over the world, in similar vessels hovering above key buildings and centres of power.

There is a brief pause, like the skip of a heartbeat, before things start falling out of the apertures. They are corpses, human corpses. The first specks of this human rain turn into a torrent, and a hideous pitter-patter grows in volume, a crashing sound on the leaded roofs, on the grassy verges, on the stone porticoes. Aylett continues:

> *Hundreds of blacks murdered in police cells hit the roof of Scotland Yard. Thousands of slaughtered East Timorese were dumped over the Assembly buildings in Jakarta. Thousands killed in the test bombings at Hiroshima and Nagasaki began raining over the Pentagon.*

Aylett's gruesome vision features an astrophysicist, Professor Skychum, who has realized that the world is being infected by a 'psychic pollution', the overflow from the cesspits of human evil. He witnesses the falling bodies from the vantage of the 8.20

Amtrak train, heading north out of Central Station, New York City. He notes that Amtrak has a policy of not stopping for bodies on the line. As he looks out of the train window and recognizes that he was right about the psychic pollution all along, he mutters to himself: 'Many happy returns.'

An ethical message

We are not living in end times as cosmology would have it. Our star, the Sun, is gradually burning down, though it's only halfway through its life and has a few billion years to go yet. Similarly, the universe may come to a close in 'heat death', the slow, slow thinning of matter and energy until the substance of space–time is so tenuous as to almost not exist. But it's a long way off. So the interest that eschatological literature has in the end times is to do with physical closure. Its calamities contain an ethical message, one of moral destruction or completion, depending upon what the gods, or nature, return. The apocalypse is an event of such momentousness that only it will do for the narrator to project the full weight of their moral seriousness on to. Predicting or writing about the end times is an expression of moral rage. It is for this reason that eschatology becomes more popular at times when people feel under terminal pressure. The end times are like an ornate mirror that reflects back to us the worst in human nature. These myths are for us now, in part acting like a memento mori, in part speaking of the desire for moral judgement. This is often depicted as a separation, from the literal meaning of the ancient Greek word for judgement – the division that will be made between the good and the bad, the true and the false, the virtuous and the evil.

Apocalyptic imagery fills the human psyche when human beings fail to feel at home in the world.

We enjoy the genre today. Many feel as though we are living in end times of a kind, be they ecological or economic or some combination of the two. It was a feature of modernity observed by Carl Jung. Living through the first half of the twentieth century, he witnessed two world wars and the rise of totalitarianism. After the wars were over, the violence was perpetuated by the threats of the Cold War and the ultimate destruction of nuclear destruction. He argued that apocalyptic imagery fills the human psyche when human beings fail to feel at home in the world. It is as if everything is turning against them, and when that mentality takes hold, it easily becomes a reality. Jung died 50 years ago, but he would no doubt argue that Byatt's and Aylett's stories are symptomatic of times in which people still feel deeply out of sorts.

I suspect that this is part of why Harold Camping achieved his moment of fame. His prophecy allowed readers of the story to stare this widespread sense of doom in the face. For a minute, we shivered, sensing that we might not be saved. But then came a kind of catharsis. The end didn't come: 21 May became 22 May. We were still living. Camping provided us with a chuckle at his expense and a collective sigh of relief. Some atheist groups reportedly held mocking after-Rapture parties, though really they were mocking themselves too. Why would they celebrate if they didn't feel, at some level, that they had got away with it?

Apocalypse stories

Traditions of eschatology – literally 'last things' – are various by definition: who knows just what will happen? Being about the end of history, they trade in myths, those stories and visions whose force and appeal rests on their ability to express, as opposed to diagnose, human fears of death and extinction, human hopes for life and salvation. They don't tell of specific details, so it is a mistake to interpret them literally. They reveal effects, like the disturbed images of a troubling dream; apocalypse means 'unveiling'. Similarly, their prophecy is not primarily concerned with future calendar dates, for all they speak of what is to come, but rather with casting a shadow across the present.

Buddhist eschatological conceptions reach for the time when the current Buddha's teachings, the Dharma, have lost their potency on Earth. The 'disappearance of learning' will be accompanied by apocalyptic signs. The oceans will shrink. There will be weeping. Monks will moderate their ascetic practices and take care of wives and children. The myth goes that a bodhisattva called Maitreya will become the next Buddha. He will rejuvenate the Dharma, and teach the world afresh about virtue and vice.

Or consider Islam. On one corner of the grand Umayyad Mosque in Damascus, Syria, stands the so-called Jesus Minaret. According to a hadith, the Prophet had a vision of Jesus descending. A local tradition developed that he will appear at the minaret on Judgement Day.

This is just one element in the complex of Muslim speculations on the last things. It is said that the armies of Gog and Magog, representing fire and flood, will lay the earth to waste. 'Mainstream Shi'ite beliefs about the end of time revolve around the notion of the twelfth imam', explains Abdulaziz Sachedina in *Islam: A Short Guide to the Faith*.

> *This 'Hidden' imam is regarded as the promised messianic Mahdi, whose return to launch the final revolution that will establish the kingdom of God on Earth is awaited by his followers. By being hidden or in 'occultation', the imam is incognito, but nevertheless still physically present.*

Together with Jesus, the Mahdi will precipitate the Battle of Armageddon, the ultimate defeat of the Antichrist and victory for God's justice. There's the hope: good will survive ill.

The feel of the Muslim tradition is not unlike that of the Christian, particularly as found in the last book of the Bible, the Revelation of St John the Divine. The poet Kathleen Norris, in an introduction to it, has called this central work of Christian apocalypticism 'a casebook of visionary excess', what with its beasts rising out of the sea, sharp two-edged swords emerging from human mouths, trumpets, thrones, the whore of Babylon and the four horses of the apocalypse.

Like Byatt's Norse myths and Aylett's short story, the biblical apocalypse is widely understood to be a comment on

contemporary events.
John sat in his cave on the
Greek island of Patmos and
contemplated the impact
of the Roman empire on
the still new movement
called Christianity. On one
level, the followers of Jesus
were being persecuted. The
infamous number of the
beast, 666, was probably a
reference to the emperor
Nero, or a subsequent
emperor, depending upon
when the book was written.
But on another level, the
book of Revelation is a
warning to Christians too.
It describes messages being
sent out to churches in
various cities across the

THE VISION OF DEATH (C. 1868) BY GUSTAVE DORÉ.

Mediterranean world. Their commitment seems to be waning; the
truth of the gospel is diluting. Revelation warns Christians against
being 'lukewarm'. It sounds not unlike the Buddhist concern
about the loss of knowledge of the Dharma.

Successful books of apocalypse encapsulate something
timeless too. In her introduction, Norris cites Mary Gaitskill, the
American novelist, who notes how the book of Revelation reads
like 'a terrible abstract of how we violate ourselves and others
and thus bring down endless suffering on earth'. But if they bring
timeless judgement, they offer timeless hope too. Norris admits to
loving St John's vision because for all the horror, it begins and ends
with a blessing on those who read it. After all the troubles, a new
song will be heard, as every tear is wiped away from every eye.

This rather beautiful side emphasizes the extraordinary
nature of being alive at all. Emily Dickinson called the book

of Revelation her favourite for this reason. It reminded her of the brilliance of life. In a letter of 1873, she wrote, 'To live is Endowment. It puts me in mind of that singular Verse in Revelation – "Every Several Gate was of one Pearl".' There is a unity in that one pearl, so that whilst shaped by suffering, the end times also carry a promise of unity, the collective feeling characteristic of a wartime spirit. We are in this together. The philosopher Friedrich Nietzsche recognized this unifying force:

> *Every culture that has lost myth has lost, by the same token, its natural healthy creativity. Only a horizon ringed about with myths can unify a culture. The forces of imagination and the Apollonian dream are saved only by myth from indiscriminate rambling.*

But there is danger. Apocalypse must be depicted as a kind of violent purification with fire. Only that can match the evil with which it is obsessed. The burning, purging of eschatological judgement therefore inevitably raises the dangerous power of apocalyptic thinking, the temptation to interpret the end time literally and to bring it on.

Redemptive violence

For some believers, it seems a small step to move from the faith that God will judge everyone at the end of time to wanting to precipitate Armageddon now. The underlying dynamic here is one of purification through violence. If the myths of eschatology almost invariably incorporate rivers of blood, then perhaps 'shock and awe' can be deployed by human beings in order to force heaven to appear on Earth now. The historian of ideas John Gray has interpreted the history of human warfare as having much to do with this desire to transform society by redemptive violence.

If you control the end, you control it all. If you've seen the end, you've seen it all.

> *For over 200 years the early Christian faith in an End-Time initiated by God was turned into a belief that Utopia could be achieved by human action. Clothed in science, early Christian myths of Apocalypse gave rise to a new kind of faith-based violence.*

In his book *Black Mass*, Gray argues that apocalyptic thinking has shaped the policies of democratic leaders like America's George W. Bush and autocratic leaders like Iran's Mahmoud Ahmadinejad alike. Aside from the personal beliefs of such politicians, eschatological policies are also a way of attempting to master events that otherwise feel as though they are running out of control. If you control the end, you control it all. If you've seen the end, you've seen it all.

Aside from politics, there is the temptation to interpret the literature literally in a spiritual sense too. In the Buddhist tradition, a tenth-century Chinese monk, commonly depicted in statues of the Laughing Buddha, is said to be one incarnation of Maitreya. More recently, the Theosophical movement of Madame Blavatsky adopted Maitreya in the nineteenth century, perhaps because the bodhisattva appears in the second section of the hugely popular *Tibetan Book of the Dead*. An important incarnation was declared again at the turn of the twentieth century in an Indian boy called Jiddu Krishnamurti, who lived next door to the Theosophical headquarters in Madras.

As for Harold Camping, he is but a recent example in a long line of Christian apocalyptic literalists, though his failure displays another aspect of the pedantry too. What happens when the predictions don't come true?

Spiritualizing Judgement Day

Camping explained his Judgement Day that never was by declaring it an invisible Judgement Day. He had come to understand it as a spiritual rather than physical event. This is a wise move, and one that quite possibly reaches back to Jesus himself. If the conclusions of modern biblical scholarship are right, the first Christians believed along with Jesus that the world was soon to come to an end. It didn't happen, but instead of abandoning the belief, the Christians spiritualized it. The end of the world was reinterpreted as the eventual completion of all things, or the coming of the kingdom, to be strived for by believers on Earth as much as brought about by God in heaven.

It is easy to laugh at the apparent cop-out. It's a mug's game: you have to chose a time for the end that is near in order to get across the message that it is the present time that is found wanting. But how many prophets have predicted the end of time, only to have their dates surpassed, their futurology proven false? When will they learn? However, the spiritualizing move conveys a great truth that is also very useful.

We humans need goals and utopias to inspire us and keep us on the right path. We will never reach that perfection – and are lucky ever to glimpse it – but the dream that it will come about motivates us profoundly. This means that predictions that don't come to pass are disconfirmed but they are not discredited. New stories keep coming because of the undiminishing human desire to comment on what is going wrong now, and to keep on hoping that one day all will be well. The Messiah will come.

It is not just religious people who recognize the value of such an attitude. It is what the French philosopher Jacques Derrida called 'messianism', an attitude that helps us to keep waiting and hoping for all manner of invaluable qualities, like justice, which the legal system, say, never quite delivers though always aspires to; or happiness, which is always fouled up by events.

So here is one last thought on the last things. Recognizing that utopian dreams of judgement or completion are always delayed means that human beings might be less likely to kill others in the name of the utopias they believe can be precipitated by acts of war or terror. Examples of such slaughter litter human history. If the perpetrators had had the sense to follow the first Christians, and spiritualize their hopes, many lives might have been saved.

IS THERE LIFE AFTER DEATH?

When religions don't teach immortality and the survival of the soul

*H*as science done it for the soul? Is an immortal soul, and therefore life after death, akin to fairies and angels and other superstitious fantasies, implausible in the modern world? It might seem that there is really only one option for anyone who takes biology seriously, the option expressed so powerfully by Francis Crick, one of the discoverers of DNA: '"You", your joys and your sorrows, your memories and ambitions, your sense of personal identity and free will, are in fact no more than the behaviour of a vast assembly of nerve cells and their associated molecules.' To be a self is to be an assembly of cells, not a creature with a soul.

I suspect that there is still currency in the notion of the soul. It does not explain what it is to be human, but I shall try to argue that it is a useful concept because it helps keep an eye on the mystery of what it is to be human, a mystery misplaced by the biologist's reduction to a chemical soup of joys and sorrows, memories and ambitions, identity and free will. But before getting to that, and the possibility of immortality, we need to take a step back and ask a slightly different question. Do religious traditions confess belief in life after death anyway?

Theories of immortality

Some do, particularly those from the East. In Hinduism, the atman is the true or real self. 'Atman' comes from the word for breath, hence the spiritual significance of breathing exercises in yogic and meditative practices. The atman is envisaged as a reflection of the Brahman, a transpersonal and universal soul into which everything merges. Nothing that is is not Brahman. So everything that is finds its fulfilment in Brahman, and in particular the atman or self finds its rightful spiritual union with the Absolute through love and devotion. This will happen after many rebirths or cycles of *samsara*. And this continuous flow is immortal, in the sense that life does not begin with birth and end with death, but is a perpetual, if shifting, stream.

However, the Western traditions that fall within the ambit of the Abrahamic religions see things rather differently. In fact, it can come as something of a surprise to learn not only that conceptions of immortality and the soul vary widely, but that some faiths do not hold out much hope of it at all.

Take ancient Judaism – the Judaism of the Hebrew Bible. Here, there is no developed notion of immortality or the soul. When it comes to what happens after death, humans are said to go to 'sheol', an ill-defined subterranean abode where the dead linger in a shadowy existence. It is a gloomy subsistence, common in the ancient Mediterranean world, and sheol itself is typically used poetically, to draw a contrast with the activities, delights and beauties of the world of the living. Life in this pit is hardly worth the name, and the Bible implies that life continues fully in the community called the people of Israel. Hence, Judaism generally stresses the importance of this life over the possibility of the next.

Another interesting thing to note is that all the dead, whether they've been good or bad in this life, drift into this half-life. It is only later that a more familiar idea develops, that of the wicked going to Gehenna, a fiery place of punishment.

In relation to the soul, human beings are said to have *nephesh* in the Jewish tradition. This translates as 'life' or 'breath', though it can be a little misleadingly translated as 'soul'. So, God is said to breathe life into the nostrils of Adam in Genesis.

Alternatively, blood can be said to be nephesh because it is the blood that contains life. Judaism might be said to have a loosely materialistic conception of what it is to be alive. It is not that we have a spiritual bit and a bodily bit, and the spiritual bit might leave the body behind after death. Rather, life is that which animates the material stuff of which we are made.

In post-biblical Judaism, the hope of everlasting life does become more prominent. However, it is different from immortality. The dead are dead. The body rots and returns to the earth, a process that is symbolically represented by corpses often being buried in contact with the ground, rather than in a coffin. But there is also an expectation of a messianic age when death will be conquered. 'He maketh death to vanish in life eternal', says an Orthodox prayer, because the dead will be resurrected. In this, modern Judaism is similar to Christianity. Both teach an identity between this life and resurrected life, though it is impossible to say just how that continuity will be achieved. Will we know a redeemed version of our thoughts and deeds, habits and character from this life? Will we return at the age at which we died, some ideal age, or will the world to come be ageless? It is impossible to say, most teachers insist, for the hope of resurrection ultimately rests with faith in God and faith in God alone.

Aristotle's conception of the soul

What this means is that in much Christian theology, the concept of the soul is not contemplated in relation to the question of life after death so much as in relation to the question of what it is to be human. The concept is borrowed from the philosophy of Aristotle. He had a straightforward starting point – not 'Is there a part of me that floats off when I die?' but, simply, 'How do the living differ from those things in the world that are not alive?' (The Latin for 'soul' helps here: *anima*. It means that which gives life, or animates.) Aristotle's key idea can be summed up in this formula: the soul is the form of a living body.

What he means emerges by considering an analogy with an item that is not living – say, a candle, made of wax. Wax of itself

> *The concept of the soul is not contemplated in relation to the question of life after death so much as in relation to the question of what it is to be human.*

can exist in all manner of undifferentiated lumps. It is only when it is fashioned into the shape of a candle, and supplied with a wick, that it can be called a candle. The wax is now a candle because it has a candle's form, Aristotle would say. Conversely, once the candle is burnt, its form ceases too, and any remaining wax assumes a stumpy formlessness once more.

The candle is not living, of course. But in the analogy, the form of the candle corresponds to the soul of a living creature. If form enables function, the soul enables life. Immediately some crucial details about the concept of the soul emerge.

By this definition, the soul does not and cannot exist apart from the body. Staying with the candle analogy, there is no form of candles that exists that is not embodied in wax. Neither, according to Aristotle, can a free-floating soul inhabit just any old body, any more than a candle could be made out of wood or water. The nature of the body crucially determines the nature of the life, quite as much as the soul.

Similarly, Aristotle argued that the soul of a human being has no life unless it is manifest in the fleshy structures we call a human body – with a thinking head and a beating heart, bipedal locomotion and opposable thumbs, and so on. Aristotle's human, then, is not an immortal soul encased in a meaty shrine: we are not embodied souls. Rather, we are ensouled bodies. When we die, the soul 'does not remember', as Aristotle hauntingly remarks. In this respect, he differs from his teacher, Plato, who strove to make sense of how souls might be immortal and exist apart from a body.

Aristotle thought that all living things have souls in this way. The soul of a cabbage or a slug is simply that which, in conjunction with the body, gives the cabbage or slug its defining characteristics. What differentiates human beings from cabbages or slugs – aside from our physical inability to photosynthesize or

produce slime – is that we have
intellectual souls. That means
a capacity to think abstract
thoughts and to decide freely.
I think abstractly when I make
the numerical observation that
although there were two slugs
eating my cabbages yesterday,
there are now six. I decide freely
when I vow to exterminate the
slugs. It is possible that other
animals have intellectual souls too,
say dolphins and bonobos, which
is to say that the Aristotelian
concept of the soul is not
anthropocentric.

PSYCHE RECEIVING THE FIRST KISS OF CUPID (1798) BY
FRANÇOIS PASCAL SIMON GERARD. THIS UNITY OF PSYCHE
AND CUPID IN ANCIENT THOUGHT REPRESENTS THE MARRIAGE
OF THE SOUL AND THE BODY NECESSARY FOR FULL HUMANITY.

This conception of the
soul is as useful now as it was
when Aristotle formulated it. It
addresses a fundamental feature
of life, though one that remains a deep mystery: namely what does
it mean to be alive? The concept of the soul doesn't explain that
mystery. Rather, it names it for what it is. Better that than miss the
fact that many things don't just exist in the world, but live in the
world. If you do elide the two, it becomes quite hard to articulate
the difference between existing and living, much to the detriment
of those things that are truly alive, that have soul.

Theologians such as Thomas Aquinas turned to Aristotle, aware
of the richness of the philosopher's insights. But they were faced with
a problem. They had to reconcile his perceptions with the church's
traditions. This is where we return to the issue of immortality.

Subsistence of the soul

Consider the saints. They were once ensouled bodies, bits of which
were preserved in churches as relics. The faithful venerate them
week by week. But they are now just bits of bodies. So where have

the souls of the saints gone? Do they disperse at death, like the energy of a wave when it breaks on the shore? Do they linger like ethereal incense amidst the sacred fragments? Or are they now departed and in heaven, as the church teaches? Aquinas believed that they were up above. But how did he reconcile this conviction that the saints live on with his respect for Aristotle, who denies the separate immortality of the soul?

> *When I die, all that I am in my particularity will not survive because my body will definitely not live on.*

We need to press the notion of the soul a stage further. Ask yourself again what the soul animates in relation to a human body. It characteristically gives us the capacities of thought and freedom, amongst other things – those things that add up to the features of intelligence. But, notes Aquinas, intelligence has special properties. In particular, it can exist without being embodied.

Moreover, it is not just humans that have it. Numbers hold a kind of intelligence, there being knowledge in the golden ratio or the relationship between squares and roots. And yet numbers are not embodied. Words are similar because, when not written down, they carry intangible thoughts too. In fact, you might say that words speak us as much as we speak words: is there anything that you or I say that has not been said before?

Our will seems to display similar features again. The living force that we call willpower is that which moves our living bodies, from the depths of their being. It is the soul of love, perhaps even a manifestation of a world-soul, a life force. This implies that it must have a kind of existence at least logically distinguishable from embodiment.

The technical term for this is subsistence. Further, Aquinas argued, that which subsists cannot be said to die, because it is bodies not energy that perishes – perishing being defined as a loss of form, like the candle melting into wax. Aquinas realized that people die, of course. Human bodies expire, stink and rot away.

However, he also reasoned that the energy or force called will or intelligence cannot die. He concluded that it subsists.

So what does this mean for creatures like us? We cannot leap straight to the conclusion that we have immortal souls. When I die, all that I am in my particularity will not survive because my body will definitely not live on. The body matters. Destroy my body and you destroy me. When I die, and if something close to a soul survives, that means that I as I was when alive do not survive. 'My soul is not I', as Aquinas puts it. If the analysis is right, I do not automatically survive death as if the essence of me leaves my dead body like a ship leaving port.

However, there is also a sense in which not everything that I was will be extinguished, because life is also a kind of animate energy, an intellect, a will – those aspects that add up to what can be called the things of the soul. We can even appreciate the timeless things of the mind, and have a taste for the transcendent, a sense of eternity in time (see *What is the Literal Meaning of Scripture?*).

Aquinas is able to go a step further. As a Christian, he took the biblical discussions of life after death seriously, and noticed something in them that is often overlooked today. St Paul and the writers of the Gospels do not believe in the immortality of the soul straightforwardly either. Rather, they hold out the hope of the resurrection of the body. Like the Jewish hope, this is the conviction that the soul is reunited with a body after death. Then, the individual can hope to live again, and being an ensouled body once more, live with everything that makes him or her a person.

There's more. Aquinas suspected that the human soul longs for a body like the dry desert longs for the rain. It does so because the body enables it to desire all manner of delights and pleasures that the soul of itself could not enjoy. This is why, he continued, the happiness of the angels in heaven is different from the happiness of the saints. Angels don't have human bodies. Their joy at the vision of God is complete, but the saint experiences a happiness that is wider in extent. It is embodied.

The resurrected body

How this all comes to pass, Aquinas does not explain. Ultimately, he is a man of faith, not science. He no more claims to know what happens when the saints are resurrected than the Bible tries to explain what happened when Jesus was raised. In fact, the biblical accounts of Easter Sunday and the weeks that followed are strange. If anything, they are anti-explanations. Sometimes Jesus's new body functions like the old. Thomas could have stuck his fingers into it. It can consume fish. Aquinas wonders whether it contained blood, and black and yellow bile.

However, Jesus also appears in the room though the doors are locked, a trick that no normal body can do. And he can be with his disciples – on one occasion walking alongside them for several miles – though they do not recognize him until they sit down to eat and he breaks bread and blesses it. The tomb is empty, which is to say that the old body is gone. But the nature of the new body is mysterious. Mary Magdalene is told not to touch it. It is like the old, in so far as she recognizes her teacher and friend when he calls her name. But it is also oddly different.

Talk of resurrected bodies might seem archaic or ridiculous, perhaps; fine if you can trust in God to perform the miraculous transformation. However, it is striking how persistent the hope of a new body remains.

Consider the amount of money and time we spend trying to renew the old bodies that we do have. Rejuvenating creams, personal trainers, clothes design, body insurance, plastic surgery, virtual reality. I wonder what percentage of the consumer economy is based on a secular, this-worldly version of Easter? Resurrection is still a pervasive hope, in secular guise.

Other resurrection-like activities occupy resources and attention too. One is the hope being placed in computers to provide us with an everlasting habitation. This is the possibility that we might, one day soon, be able to upload ourselves into a mainframe and live for ever, so long as no one pulls the plug.

The speculation rests on what is referred to as the Omega Point theory, or the Singularity. The power of microprocessors will increase without limit, the theory goes, with the concomitant result that the amount of information the future will be able to handle will effectively reach infinity. This means that everything that has been, that is and that will be will fall within the reach of human beings, or whatever entities succeed us as our evolutionary path unfolds. With such omniscience, resurrection will follow, for what are our lives if not complex churns of information? the Singularity creed teaches. As the physicist Frank Tipler puts it, in his book *The Physics of Immortality*: 'If any reader has lost a loved one, or is afraid of death, modern physics says: "Be comforted, you and they shall live again."'

Tipler is far from alone in expressing hopes like this. The Singularity Institute in California is influential in the visions espoused by hi-tech companies like Google. However, theologians have critiqued this new religion.

The Christian view is that life is not a processing of information. It is the animated phenomenon of the ensouled body. Similarly, resurrected life would not be a continuation of this one, only with bigger databanks and faster toys. Rather, it must be made entirely new. After all, what is the attraction of more and more and more of basically the same life, extended indefinitely into the future? The joys of life would continue, for sure, but so would the worries, the pains, the agonies. Further, if the pleasures of life were amplified on silicon, perhaps the ills would be too. Resurrection, then, is not the same as replication. Hence, the resurrected body depicted in the Bible is as unlike the physical body as a fully grown plant is unlike a seed.

> *Resurrection, then, is not the same as replication.*

There is a deeper objection to the supercomputer hope for more and more life too. Behind it lies the assumption that we are machines. The experience of being human is envisaged as the by-product of brain activity. Therefore, so long as you can replicate

> *The soul helps check the tendency to collapse life into the behaviour of a vast blind assembly of cells.*

the brain activity, you can extend the life. The firing of neurons is aligned to the firing of silicon chips.

But that does not seem right. If it were so, then the electronics inside your computer would mean that the computer was experiencing itself, much as we experience ourselves, if to a lesser degree. If you really believed that to be so, you might think twice before shutting your computer down or commanding it to open a new application. Maybe it doesn't want to be turned off or spend hours poring over yet another spreadsheet?

That the thought is ridiculous highlights the fact that existing is different from living. It's Aristotle's main point again. A computer has a body. It does not have a soul. Therein lies every difference.

The best thing in us

Aristotle's ideas are helpful and, to me, persuasive. 'We must not heed those who advise us to think as human beings since we are human and to think mortal things since we are mortal', he urges his followers, 'but we must be like immortals in so far as possible and do everything toward living in accordance with the best thing in us.' This side of the grave, we are definitely mortals, he argues, and so advises a certain humility, to be like immortals in so far as is possible. But we are also ensouled bodies. Even if an afterlife is hard to accept, with what we know about human biology, that seems to be no reason to give up on 'the best thing in us'. And that best thing is well captured by the word 'soul'.

INDEX

Page numbers in *italic* denote an illustration

PICTURE CREDITS

Quercus Publishing Plc
55 Baker Street
7th Floor, South Block
London, W1U 8EW

First published in 2012

UK and associated territories:
ISBN 978 1 78087 032 8

Canada:
ISBN 978 1 84866 193 6

Edited by Jane Selley
Designed by Patrick Nugent
Picture research by Emma O'Neill

Printed and bound in China

10 9 8 7 6 5 4 3 2 1